A Fire
That
Burns
but
Does
Not
Consume:

D1007860

Devotions for
Thoughtful Christians

There the angel of the Lord appeared to him in flames of fire from within a bush. Moses saw that though the bush was on fire it did not burn up. Exodus 3:2

James P. Stobaugh
For Such a Time as This Ministries
Hollsopple, Pennsylvania

Acknowledgments

I wish to thank Mrs. Judy Kovalik, Dr. David Garber, and Mr. Jim Butti for their editorial assistance. I also want to thank my professors at Harvard University, Princeton Theological Seminary, and Gordon Conwell Seminary who introduced me to "a fire that burns but does not consume."

Scripture text is from The Holy Bible, *New International Version* ®, Copyright © 1973, 1978, 1984 by the International Bible Society, and is used by permission of Zondervan Publishing House, with all rights reserved. Other "Credits, Permissions, and Sources" are listed at the back of the book.

A FIRE THAT BURNS BUT DOES NOT CONSUME: DEVOTIONS FOR THOUGHTFUL CHRISTIANS
Copyright © 2003 by James P. Stobaugh
Published by For Such A Time As This Ministries
Printed in the United States of America
Book design by James P. Stobaugh
Cover design by James Butti

Printed in the United States of America.
International Standard Book Number: 0-9725890-9-0
10 9 8 7 6 5 4 3 2 1   11 10 09 08 07 06 05 04 03 02

This Book is gratefully dedicated to
my wife Karen
whose passion for God has changed a man, a
family, and a nation.

Preface

At the beginning of the 21st century Christians must be clever and resourceful. "His intent was that now, through the church, the manifold wisdom of God should be made known to the rulers and authorities in the heavenly realms, according to his eternal purpose which he accomplished in Christ Jesus our Lord " (Ephesians 3:10-11). However, it is no longer good enough to be smart. Christians must be fighters. They must be fighters *now* because they are in a culture war. This culture war will be won or lost by those who know how to fight well.

To be successful in any campaign one must know the enemy. The enemy of the people of God is not flesh and blood. It is the spirit of this age, powers and principalities. It is incipient mediocrity that threatens the very underpinnings of modern civilization.

This enemy is overcome by alacrity, not by manipulation, by good, not by evil. The weapons are the whole armor of God (Ephesians 6). Christians must know who they are in Christ. As a point of fact, they are more than conquerors (Romans 8:37). But they need to act like it.

It is the prayer of this author that these devotions will help Christians assume their rightful place in the Kingdom. They will equip them with the ammunition they need to overcome the Enemy.

This book will take readers on a year-long journey from the beginning of Western philosophy to the present. Readers will examine a philosopher or a philosophical movement and, then, they will look at a biblical refutation of the deception or a complement to the truth. Each devotional will invite participants to pray based on Scripture passages so readers will not merely be talking *about* spiritual warfare, they will be *engaged in* spiritual warfare. Each section will end with an invitation to pray similar Scriptures for the remainder of the week.

There is pathos and tragedy in this book. From the Ionian Anaximander to the Existential Viktor Frankl, many great thinkers have seen a part, but few have seen the whole truth and counsel of God. Most have failed to grasp the Good News that is so simply presented in the Word of God, the Logos, υῶεῶ. Some missed all the truth. Some discovered part of the truth. Not one recognized the whole truth. Ultimately their search proved futile. Jesus Christ--not a philosophical principle, not a metaphysical reality, not a phenomenological moment--is the Way, the Truth, the Life (John 14: 6).

Nonetheless, Christians can read this book with hope and assurance. They know Jesus Christ has triumphed over all things. They know absolutely that every knee shall bow, every tongue confess that Jesus Christ is Lord (Phil. 2:10-11).

This is no small comfort to Christian warriors. As they study and pray their way through this book they observe the great culture war of the 21st century unfold. John Jefferson Davis, Ph. D., home schooling father of five children, in his book *Evangelical Ethics* (1993) includes the following quote from Dr. Robert Foote of Cornell University. "I am reminded of a story," Dr. Robert Foote says, "where the pilot says, 'This is your captain speaking. We are flying at an altitude of 35,000 feet and the speed of 700 miles and hour. We have some good news and some bad news. The bad news is that we are lost. The good news is that we are making excellent time.'"

Dr. Foote's characterization of the modern world captures the dilemma 21st century people are facing: there is no doubt that we are making significant progress on all epistemological fronts, but at the same time we seem to be lost. It does not take a Harvard-educated sociologist to see that modern culture is in big trouble. As this new millennium begins, out-of-control individualism and egalitarianism are everywhere evident. One merely has to recall the United States' impeachment hearings several years ago. The self-proclaimed moral position of "if what I am doing harms no one (individualism) then it is OK to do it (egalitarianism)" is dominating the moral universe. Modern culture is a therapeutic culture, where holiness is replaced by wholeness, sanctification is replaced by therapy. One bright spot is that even the most committed pagans are getting truly tired of this dysfunctional culture!

> It is now questionable whether modern cultural order is capable of nourishing the freedom, responsibility, and civility that people require to sustain vital lives.

Many Christian apologists warn us that at some point people will become fed up with the excesses and dysfunctional aspects of our culture. They say that as modern mainline culture fails to sustain people in their hedonistic pursuit of self-interest, they will want something more. This culture of hopelessness and superfluity is evidenced in the billboards that line highways, in the songs that play on radios, in the movies that entertain in theaters. Culture is exemplified in university courses, in the best-seller list. It is now questionable whether modern cultural order is capable of nourishing the freedom, responsibility, and civility that people require to sustain vital lives. Modernity (a word to describe modern culture) creates problems far deeper than drugs. It creates a crisis of cultural authority in which beliefs, ideals, and traditions are losing their compelling force in society. There is a numbness spreading across the land that presents much opportunity for Christians.

This author intends for Christians to make the most of these opportunities. Christians should be encouraged that in the near future people will be looking to places of stability and strength for direction. By default, those Christians whose lives are in reasonably good shape, who have some reason to live beyond the next paycheck will have an irresistible appeal. In fact, there has not been a greater time for hope since the time of Augustine of Hippo, at the end of the Roman Empire. In the face of unspeakable horror and persecution that was everywhere manifested in the barbarian hordes, Augustine called his Christian brothers and sisters to live victorious, hopeful lives. In a modest way, that is the purpose of this book–it invites and equips Christians to prosper in an inhospitable culture. Augustine understood that Christians must stake their claim to their citizenship in the city of God. Many did. As a result, while the barbarians conquered Rome, the Christians conquered the barbarians. Within one generation Christianity became the predominant world view of Western Europe. While living in a hostile culture, Christians must prepare to live and to thrive in the city of God. Christians must with vitality and readiness live in the world without succumbing to the world's system (John 15:19).

> Christians should be encouraged that in the near future people will be looking to places of stability and strength for direction. They will look to Christ.

To this hopeless, secular world, history is mundane; it is merely utilitarian. To the Christian, history is sacred, wrought with opportunity. To secular people history is not didactic; it helps people feel better. To the Christian, history is full of important lessons, and it challenges people to be all they can be in Christ. To secular people, time and space are finite entities full of fearful pitfalls. To the Christian, no matter how bad things are, because God is alive and well, time is holy and the land is holy. Secular people act out of no purpose or design. In contrast, Christians know that God is in absolute control of history. In a way that is not mawkish or condescending, Christians must be tirelessly hopeful. Christians do that by speaking the truth found in the Word of God in places of deception.

These devotions, then, are ammunition for the faithful as they fight the good fight, run the good race (Hebrews 12:1-2). As Christians confront the Enemy they must show no mercy. As the fight proceeds, and victory inevitably follows, it is the hopeful prayer of this author that this book will contribute in some meaningful if modest way to the resounding revival that shall surely come in the next few years.

Overview

Week	Philosopher/ Philosophy	Texts	
1	**Greek Mythology** The Greeks introduced the idea that the universe was orderly, that man's senses were valid and, as a consequence, that man's proper purpose was to live his own life to the fullest.	Day 1 Day 2 Day 3 Day 4 Day 5 Day 6 Day 7	Isaiah 6:1-3 Psalm 68:13 Proverbs 11:23 Psalm 24:3-5 Micah 6:8 2 Corinthians 7:1 1 Corinthians 3: 16, 17
2	**Ionian School (500 B.C.)** The Ionian fascination with the physical world anticipated later discussions in Western philosophy.	Day 1 Day 2 Day 3 Day 4 Day 5 Day 6 Day 7	Genesis 1:1-2 Leviticus 20:26 Malachi 2:10 Hebrews 2:7 Psalm 8:6-8 Psalm 33:13-15 2 Corinthians 4: 6, 7, 16
3	**The Phythagoreans (530 B.C.)** Phythagoras was the first philosopher to require some standard of behavior from his followers. One can imagine what a novel and important step this was–that a religion would require a commitment from its adherents.	Day 1 Day 2 Day 3 Day 4 Day 5 Day 6 Day 7	James 1:22-25 1 John 2:4 Deuteronomy 29: 18-19 Job 15:31 Psalm 20: 7-8 Amos 6:1, 3, 13 Galatians 6:7-8
4	**The Eleatic School (500 B.C.)** The Eleatic School argued that reality was indivisible and endless.	Day 1 Day 2 Day 3 Day 4 Day 5 Day 6 Day 7	Peter 1:18-23 Psalm 46:4 1 Chronicles 16:35 Psalm 107:9 Isaiah 1:18 Matthew 1:21 Galatians 1:4

5	**The Pluralists** **(500 B.C.)** With no outside force in place, by chance the universe evolved from chaos to structure, and vice versa, in an eternal cycle.	Day 1 Day 2 Day 3 Day 4 Day 5 Day 6 Day 7	Genesis 1:24-25 2 Corinthians 5:17 Nehemiah 9:6 Job 26:7 Psalm 102:25 Acts 14:15 Hebrews 11:3
6	**The Sophists** **(500 B.C.)** Ethical rules needed to be followed only when it was to one's practical advantage to do so. Goodness, morality, and ethics were a reflection of culture rather than vice versa.	Day 1 Day 2 Day 3 Day 4 Day 5 Day 6 Day 7	John 3:16 Isaiah 45:9 Romans 9:20-21 Psalm 57:7 2 Thesssalonians 3:3 Revelation 22:11 Psalm 108:1
7	**Socrates** **(469-399 B.C.)** For the first time, the importance of human language was advanced by a philosopher.	Day 1 15 Day 2 Day 3 Day 4 Day 5 Day 6 Day 7	Ecclesiastes 1:13- Philippians 3:12-15 Colossians 2:9-11 Colossians 3:14 Psalm 18:32 Proverbs 2:21 Deuteronomy 5:32
8	**Plato** **(428 B.C.-?)** Plato stressed the intellectual basis of virtue, identifying virtue with wisdom.	Day 1 Day 2 Day 3 Day 4 Day 5 Day 6 Day 7	John 8:12 Psalm 27:1 Psalm 119:105 Isaiah 58:8 Isaiah 60:19-20 John 3:19-21 John 9:5
9	**Plato** **(428 B.C.-?)** "Love" to Plato was a "form" from which virtue flowed.	Day 1 Day 2 Day 3 Day 4 Day 5 Day 6 Day 7	1 Corinthians 13 John 17:26 John 17:23 Deuteronomy 10:12 Deuteronomy 7:9 2 John 6 Jude 21

10	**Aristotle** **(350 B.C.-?)** Aristotle was the first agnostic. Aristotle argued that reality lay in empirical, measurable knowledge.	Day 1	Romans 3:12
		Day 2	Psalm 120: 2, 5-7
		Day 3	Proverbs 8:13
		Day 4	Amos 3:2-3
		Day 5	Hebrews 12:14
		Day 6	Proverbs 10:23
		Day 7	James 5:16
11	**Aristotle** **(350 B.C.-?)** Aristotle, for the first time discussed the gods as if they were quantified entities. He spoke about them as if they were not present.	Day 1	Genesis 3:1-3
		Day 2	Joshua 1:8
		Day 3	Deuteronomy 2:7
		Day 4	Deuteronomy 1:10
		Day 5	Exodus 23:22
		Day 6	1 Peter 3:12-13
		Day 7	Luke 18:7-8
12	**Cynicism** **(350 B.C.)** For the first time, philosophers began to talk about the individual in earnest, as if he were a subject to be studied.	Day 1	Ecclesiastes 12:6-8
		Day 2	John 7:38
		Day 3	Luke 11:33-36
		Day 4	John 11:25-26
		Day 5	Philippians 4:6-7
		Day 6	1 John1:9
		Day 7	1 John 5:14
13	**Skepticism** **(300 B. C.)** Skepticism maintained that human beings could know nothing of the real nature of things, and that consequently the wise person would give up trying to know anything.	Day 1	Romans 8:28-30
		Day 2	John 5:24
		Day 3	John 10:27-29
		Day 4	John 11:25-26
		Day 5	Psalm 90:12
		Day 6	Psalm 90:17
		Day 7	Psalm 118:24
14	**Epicurianism** **(300 B. C.)** The aim of human life, Epicurus claimed, was to achieve maximum pleasure with the least effort and risk.	Day 1	Galatians 2:20
		Day 2	Psalm 84:10-12
		Day 3	Psalm 77:11-12
		Day 4	Psalm 73:28
		Day 5	Psalm 32:11
		Day 6	Psalm 42:8
		Day 7	Psalm 31:24

15	**Stoicism** **(300 B.C.)** Stoicism celebrated the human spirit and it became the measuring rod against which all social and religious institutions were measured.	Day 1 Day 2 Day 3 Day 4 Day 5 Day 6 Day 7	Matthew 5:3-12 Matthew 10:29 2 Corinthians 9:8-10 Philippians 4:19 1 Chronicles 17:27 Matthew 6:11 3 John 2
16	**Neoplatonism** **(A.D. 50)** Neoplatonism dared to speak of a religious experience as a philosophical phenomenon	Day 1 Day 2 Day 3 Day 4 Day 5 Day 6 Day 7	John 1:1-3 Hebrews 1:18 2 Timothy 2:15 2 Peter 1:21 1 Corinthians 2:12 Hebrews 1:1-2 Romans 1:4
17	**Augustine** **(A.D. 354-430)** Augustine effectively articulated a theology and world view for the Church as it journeyed into the inhospitable, post-Christian, barbarian era.	Day 1 Day 2 Day 3 Day 4 Day 5 Day 6 Day 7	Psalm 48:1-2 Luke 18:1 1 Timothy 2:8 Ephesians 3:11-12 Hebrews 4:16 Jude 20 Revelation 5:8
18	**Scholasticism** **(A.D. 1100-1300)** Scholasticism, with varying degrees of success, attempted to use natural human reason--in particular, the philosophy and science of Aristotle--to understand the metaphysical content of Christian revelation.	Day 1 Day 2 Day 3 Day 4 Day 5 Day 6 Day 7	Jeremiah 9:23-24 James 3:17 1 John 2: 20, 27 2 Timothy 1:7 John 9:5, 39 1 John 5:20 Psalm 25:4-5
19	**Erasmus** **(1466-1536)** Erasmus, for the first time, discussed things like happiness as being centered in the self or personhood of the man or woman. Happiness was based on some narcissist notions of self-love.	Day 1 Day 2 Day 3 Day 4 Day 5 Day 6 Day 7	Nehemiah 8:10 Job 4:4 Psalm 18:31-33 Psalm 22:18-20 Psalm 68:34-36 Proverbs 30:24-26 Psalm 18:38-40

20	**Michel de Montaigne (1533-1592)** Montaigne reintroduced Greek skepticism to Western culture.	Day 1 Day 2 Day 3 Day 4 Day 5 Day 6 Day 7	Galatians 3: 26-28 Philippians 2:5-7 Mark 1:14-16 Luke 6:19-21 Romans 14:16-18 Hebrews 12:27-29 Revelation 1:5-7
21	**Frances Bacon (1561-1626)** Bacon advanced vigorously the idea that reasoning must triumph over theology.	Day 1 Day 2 Day 3 Day 4 Day 5 Day 6 Day 7	1 Corinthians 1:18-21 Galatians 6:13-15 Colossians 1:19-21 Colossians 2:13-16 Matthew 10:37-39 Luke 14:26-28 Ephesians 2:15-17
22	**Thomas Hobbes (1588-1679)** Hobbes was one of the first modern Western thinkers to provide a secular justification for political power.	Day 1 Day 2 Day 3 Day 4 Day 5 Day 6 Day 7	Revelation 4:10-11 Job 42:2 Psalm 139:8 Psalm 139:4 1 Corinthians 2:12 Psalm 8:1 Psalm 19:1
23	**Rene Descartes (1596-1650)** After Descartes, mankind replaced God as the center of the universe in the midst of many. This was an ominous moment in Western culture.	Day 1 Day 2 Day 3 Day 4 Day 5 Day 6 Day 7	Hebrews 2:6-8 2 Corinthians 5:9-10 2 Corinthians 4:6-7 2 Corinthians 5:6-8 John 5:24 John 6:37 John 6:51
24	**Benedictus de Spinoza (1732-1677)** Spinoza argued that human morality arose from self-interest.	Day 1 Day 2 Day 3 Day 4 Day 5 Day 6 Day 7	Exodus 20:1-17 Romans 5:18-20 Romans 6:15-17 Hebrews 4:10-12 1 Peter 1:1-3 2 John 2:5-7 Hebrews 5:7-9

25	**John Locke** **(1632-1704)** Locke believed in reasoning and common sense, rather than in metaphysics.	Day 1 Day 2 Day 3 Day 4 Day 5 Day 6 Day 7	Isaiah 59:1-3 Romans 3:23-25 1 Corinthians 1:29-31 Romans 8:22-24 Ephesians 1:13-15 Ephesians 1:6-8 Hebrews 9:11-13
26	**G. W. Leibniz** **(1646-1716)** Leibniz believed in a God who created a world separate from His sovereignty.	Day 1 Day 2 Day 3 Day 4 Day 5 Day 6 Day 7	Psalm 139:7-10 1 Corinthians 11:31-33 2 Timothy 1:6-8 Hebrews 12:6-11 Revelation 3:18-20 Titus 1:7-9 Hebrews 12:1-2
27	**George Berkeley** **(1685-1753)** Berkeley called "intuition," was the voice of God to mankind.	Day 1 Day 2 Day 3 Day 4 Day 5 Day 6 Day 7	Hebrews 4:12-13 Matthew 4:3-5 Luke 11:27-29 Ephesians 6:16-18 Colossians 3:16 Colossians 3: 17 1 Thessalonians 2:13
28	**Davie Hume** **(1711-1726)** Hume, for the first time in Western history, seriously suggested that there was no necessary connection between cause and effect.	Day 1 Day 2 Day 3 Day 4 Day 5 Day 6 Day 7	Galatians 6:6-10 Ephesians 4:7 James 5:11 2 Corinthians 7:9-11 1 Peter 2:25 Hosea 6:1 Lamentations 3:40-41
29	**Immanuel Kant** **(1724-1804)** Kant argued that reality was experience. If one could not experience something with his senses, then it was not real.	Day 1 Day 2 Day 3 Day 4 Day 5 Day 6 Day 7	Matthew 5:28-42 Psalm 26:12 Psalm 27:1-6, 13 Psalm 28: 6-8 Psalm 145:4-7, 10-12 Acts 5:31-32 Psalm 89:1

30	**Jean Jacques Rousseau (1712-1778)** Rousseau advocated one of the first "back-to-nature" movements.	Day 1 Day 2 Day 3 Day 4 Day 5 Day 6 Day 7	John 3:19-20 Psalm 69:5 Romans 3:23 Romans 6:23 John 1:12 Titus 3:5 2 Corinthians 5:21
31	**William Godwin (1756-1836)** The notion that there were individual rights, or a codex of governing laws, was anathema to Godwin.	Day 1 Day 2 Day 3 Day 4 Day 5 Day 6 Day 7	Psalm 58:3 Lamentations 3:22-23 Micah 7:7 Malachi 4:2 1 Corinthians 15:57 Psalm 138:4-6 Psalm 136:26
32	**Soren Kierkegaard (1813-1855)** Kiergegaard explained life in terms of logical necessity, became a means of avoiding choice and responsibility.	Day 1 Day 2 Day 3 Day 4 Day 5 Day 6 Day 7	Deuteronomy 13:19-20 2 Samuel 2:32-34 Psalm 27:1 1 Chronicles 16:8-12 Psalm 7:17 1 Chronicles 16:23-27 2 Samuel 22:4
33	**G. W. F. Hegel (1770-1831)** Truth had no application if there were not opposites warring for its reality.	Day 1 Day 2 Day 3 Day 4 Day 5 Day 6 Day 7	Luke 12:8-9 Psalm 71:15, 19 Judges 5:11 Ezra 9:15 Job 36:3 Psalm 5:8 Psalm 7:9
34	**Karl Marx (1818-1883)** To the Hegelian Marx, Christianity was a fairy tale created to placate weak people.	Day 1 Day 2 Day 3 Day 4 Day 5 Day 6 Day 7	Isaiah 40:28-31 Proverbs 14:19 Proverbs 19:21 Joel 2:21, 23, 26 Hosea 2:8, 21, 22 Daniel 6:20-22 Ezekiel 36:9-11, 30, 36

35	**Pierre Joseph Proudon (1809-1865)** Proudon instituted the last serious philosophical attempt to undermine the human will as a determining factor in human decision-making.	Day 1 Day 2 Day 3 Day 4 Day 5 Day 6 Day 7	Genesis 1:26-28 Job 31:15 Psalm 8:5 Psalm 100:3 Psalm 119:73 Psalm 139:14 Isaiah 64:8
36	**Arthur Schopenhauer (1788-1860)** The human will, with all its chauvinism and narcissism, was the most powerful human impulse.	Day 1 Day 2 Day 3 Day 4 Day 5 Day 6 Day 7	John 14:16-21 1 Corinthians 2:11 1 Corinthians 6:20 Romans 7:14-25 Job 9:4 Psalm 104:24 Amos 5:8
37	**Herbert Spencer (1820-1903)** Spencer argued that in biological sciences and in the social sciences the fittest and the strongest survived	Day 1 Day 2 Day 3 Day 4 Day 5 Day 6 Day 7	Genesis 6:5-7 Acts 6:4 Romans 1:9 Romans 12:12 Ephesians 1:15-16 1 Thessalonians 5:17 2 Timothy 1:3
38	**Frederich Nietzsche (1844-1890)** Nietzsche believed that the collapse of the religious impulse has left a huge vacuum. The history of modern times is in great part the history of how that vacuum is filled.	Day 1 Day 2 Day 3 Day 4 Day 5 Day 6 Day 7	Daniel 5: 25-258 2 Timothy 2:3, 22 2 Timothy 3:2-7 Hosea 6:6 Luke 4:8 1 Timothy 2:8 Revelation 15:4
39	**Martin Heidegger (1889-1976)** The meaning of the world must be discovered outside human experience.	Day 1 Day 2 Day 3 Day 4 Day 5 Day 6 Day 7	John 14:6 Psalm 150:1-6 Psalm 69:5-6 Philippians 4:8 Exodus 33:13 1 Corinthians 10:31 2 Corinthians 4:16-18

40	**Jean Paul Sartre** **(1905-1980)** People exist in a world of their own making.	Day 1 Day 2 Day 3 Day 4 Day 5 Day 6 Day 7	Romans 10:9 Psalm 71:14-17 Matthew 5:16 Matthew 7:12 Mark 10:45 1 Timothy 2:1 1 John 2: 15-16
41	**Simone De Beauvoir** **(1906-1986)** Beauvoir was an advocate of "free love" and completely rejected the biblical understanding of marriage, which she saw as an oppressive institution.	Day 1 Day 2 Day 3 Day 4 Day 5 Day 6 Day 7	Proverbs 31:26-29 Malachi 4:6 Matthew 10:37 Ephesians 6:4 1 Thessalonians 2:11 Proverbs 22: 6, 15 Proverbs 23:13-14
42	**John Dewey** **(1859-1952)** Truth to Dewey was a reflection of circumstances and contingencies.	Day 1 Day 2 Day 3 Day 4 Day 5 Day 6 Day 7	Psalm 78:4 1 John 5:3 2 Corinthians 1:3-4 2 Corinthians 4: 6-7 2 Corinthians 4: 16-18 2 Corinthians 5:6-8 2 Rointhians 5:9-10
43	**Bertrand Russell** **(1872-1970)** If an actual event could not be quantified or repeated then it was not real.	Day 1 Day 2 Day 3 Day 4 Day 5 Day 6 Day 7	Romans 5:3-5 Ezekiel 36:26-29 Romans 7:6, 24-25 Romans 12:2 1 Corinthians 1:9, 24, 30 1 Corinthians 2: 12, 14-16 1 Peter 2:3, 9
44	**John Stuart Mill** **(1806-1873)** To Mill, the individual and his needs were paramount.	Day 1 Day 2 Day 3 Day 4 Day 5 Day 6 Day 7	Galatians 5:1 Ezra 8:23 Daniel 9:3-5, 9-10 Matthew 6:9-10 Psalm 4:6 Psalm 85:4-7 Psalm 138:8

45	**Max Weber** **(1864-1920)** The notion that God was pleased with hard work and frugal living assured a healthy maturation of society	Day 1 Day 2 Day 3 Day 4 Day 5 Day 6 Day 7	1 Corinthians 9:5-7 Psalm 37:3 Psalm 90:17 Deuteronomy 6:25 Ezekiel 18:5-9 Matthew 6:1-4 Romans 2:13
46	**Ludwig Wittgenstein** **(1889-1951)** If a person could not speak it, it was not real.	Day 1 Day 2 Day 3 Day 4 Day 5 Day 6 Day 7	Revelation 21:5-7 Romans 16:25-26 Acts 2:38 Romans 10:3-9 1 Timothy 3:16 2 Timothy 1:9-10 2 Timothy 2:13-14
47	**Richard Rorty** **(1931-)** Truth to Rorty is what we all agree is truth and what we agree is truth is more a reflection of circumstances than it is any absolute or objective reality outside mankind's experience.	Day 1 Day 2 Day 3 Day 4 Day 5 Day 6 Day 7	Isaiah 6:5-8 Isaiah 32:17 Isaiah 52:1, 11 Isaiah 61:3, 9-11 1 Thessalonians 2:12 1 Thessalonians 3:13 1 Thessalonians 5:5, 22-23
48	**Alfred North Whitehead** **(1861-1947)** The agnostic Whitehead believed in God--if a decidedly anemic God.	Day 1 Day 2 Day 3 Day 4 Day 5 Day 6 Day 7	Psalm 36:5-9 Matthew 3:1-10 Matthew 18:21-35 Matthew 20:1-16 Acts 7:54-8:8 1 Kings 19:1-8 Psalm 42
49	**Jacques Derrida** **(1930-)** Derrida argued that most of us merely play language games. Every utterance is a move in a language game.	Day 1 Day 2 Day 3 Day 4 Day 5 Day 6 Day 7	Zechariah12:1-5 John 17:1-5 Romans 8:18-30 Acts 2:14, 22-24 Revelation 1:4-8 Psalm 2 John 20:19-31

50	**Jean Baudrillard** **(1929-)** Reality to Baudrillard, is not necessarily defined by human language: it is defined by the public media.	Day 1	Daniel 7:9-10
		Day 2	Exodus 16:2-15
		Day 3	Romans 11:13-16
		Day 4	Jeremiah 20;7-13
		Day 5	Psalm 10:12-18
		Day 6	Luke 12:49-56
		Day 7	Matthew 8:1-4
51	**Jurgen Habermas** **(1929-)** Habermas has resurrected the works of Plato and other metaphysicists and has taken philosophy away from language and communication and has taken it back to a discussion of rationality.	Day 1	Isaiah 1:18-19
		Day 2	Jeremiah 31:31-34
		Day 3	Hebrews 5:7-10
		Day 4	Philippians 3:8-14
		Day 5	Psalm 126
		Day 6	John 12:1-8
		Day 7	Matthew 16:21-28
52	**Viktor E. Frankl** **(1905-1997)** Man was now the result of a purposeless and materialistic process that did not have him in mind.	Day 1	Isaiah 55:8-9
		Day 2	Psalm 131:1
		Day 3	Psalm 19:13
		Day 4	Job 37:24
		Day 5	Proverbs 13:10
		Day 6	Proverbs 15:5, 10, 12, 55
		Day 7	1 Corinthians 3:18

Week 1

Greek Mythology

The ancient Greeks did not have a religion *per se*; they did not go to Sunday school and church like we do. They had no Ten Commandments or any other moral system, for that matter, to follow. Besides, hardly any self-respecting Greek really thought that mythological gods and goddesses were alive, at least not the way we think of our Judeo-Christian God. The Greek gods cared little, if they cared at all, for mankind. While it is true that Greek society had its gods, it did not place great importance on mystical beliefs. Indeed, what gods it did revere (not worship) were much different from the Christian God. In Christianity man was made "in God's image." The Greek gods were made in the image of man. They were neither omnipotent nor omnipresent. One scholar, Edith Hamilton,

> The Greeks introduced the idea that the universe was orderly, that man's senses were valid and, as a consequence, that man's proper purpose was to live his own life to the fullest.

stated, "Before Greece, all religion was magical." She further illustrated that mystical beliefs were based on fear of the unknown, whereas the Greeks "changed a world that was full of fear into a world full of beauty." Hamilton continued, "The Greeks were the first intellectuals. In a world where the irrational had played the chief role, they came forward as the protagonists of the mind." Thus, the Greeks introduced the idea that the universe was orderly, that man's senses were valid and, as a consequence, that man's proper purpose was to live his own life to the fullest. Man's chief end, however, was certainly not to please the gods. It was to enjoy the aesthetics.

Passage

The abode of the gods was on the summit of Mount Olympus, in Thessalonica. A gate of clouds, kept by the goddesses named the Seasons, opened to permit the passage of the Celestials to earth, and to receive them on their return. The gods had their separate dwellings;

but all, when summoned, came to the palace of Jupiter, as did also those deities whose usual abode was the earth, the waters, or the under-world. It was also in the great hall of the palace of the Olympian king that the gods feasted each day on ambrosia and nectar, their food and drink, the latter being handed round by the lovely goddess Hebe. Here they conversed of the affairs of heaven and earth; and as they quaffed their nectar, Apollo, the god of music, delighted them with the tones of his lyre, to which the Muses sang in responsive strains. When the sun was set, the gods retired to sleep in their respective dwellings. (*Bullfinch's Mythology*)

Biblical Response

Isaiah the prophet clarified the real status of our God.

Isaiah 6:1-3 In the year King Uzziah died, I saw the Lord. He was sitting on a lofty throne, and the train of his robe filled the Temple. Hovering around him were mighty seraphim, each with six wings. With two wings they covered their faces, with two they covered their feet, and with the remaining two they flew. In a great chorus they sang, "Holy, holy, holy is the LORD Almighty! The whole earth is filled with his glory!" (NLT)

Journaling Question:

Are there times when God seems stern and other times when he does not? Describe a time when you really needed God to be gentle and kind to you and He came through for you.

Praying Scripture

ALMIGHTY GOD, HOLY GOD, GOD WHOSE TRAIN FILLS THE TEMPLE, GOD WHOM THE SERAPHIM BOW DOWN AND WORSHIP, A GOD IN WHOSE PRESENCE THE FALSE GODS AND GODDESSES OF THIS AGE PALE IN COMPARISON, I WORSHIP AND PRAISE YOU. THE WHOLE EARTH IS FILLED WITH YOUR GLORY! AMEN.

Further Reflection

Week 2

The Ionian School   (580 B.C.)

Western philosophy grew out of discussions about ultimate things, or things that seemed really important. Thales, Anaximander, and Anaminenes, Greek philosophers living in the ancient Greek province of Iona, saw their vocation in that light. They speculated on penultimate truth. There was no demarcation between philosophy and the physical sciences. They argued that all things were created from an unknown intangible, invisible, ubiquitous substance called "apeiron." All things were made of "apeiron." This strange substance was indestructible and unlimited. It was made finite in the sense that mankind only could observe the portion that was on the earth. This early fascination with the physical world anticipated later discussions in Western philosophy. The Ionian School anticipated the modern notion of an unbounded universe created by nameless physical forces unrelated to any deity, much less to a benevolent, loving God. The Ionian philosophers piqued the interest of generations of philosophers and invited later thinkers to merge the visible and invisible world without reference to a personal, omniscient God. They were the first philosophers to suggest that material substance explained natural phenomena. It was a short skip and jump to the panoply that atheistic Carl Sagan developed in the last part of the 20th century.

> The Ionian fascination with the physical world anticipated later discussions in Western philosophy.

Passage

- Of all things that are, the most ancient is God, for he is uncreated.
- The most beautiful is Cosmos, because it is God's action.
- The larger is space, because it holds all things.
- The swiftest is mind, because it speeds everywhere
- The strongest is the necessity, for it matters all.
- The wisest is the time, because he brings everything to light.
- The things you offer to your parents you must wait to get from your children.
- There is no difference between life and death.

4

- Know thyself.
- Someone asked him which is older, day or night and he replied "Night is the older by one day."
- Someone asked him who is the happiest man and he replied "The one who has healthy body, resourceful mind and a docile nature."
  (Thales)

Biblical Response

God and His creation are forever separate. He is the creator; the universe is His creation. This is a chasm that can never be crossed.

> **Genesis 1:1-2** In the beginning God created the heavens and the earth. Now the earth was formless and empty, darkness was over the surface of the deep, and the Spirit of God was hovering over the waters.

Journal Writing

Describe a feeling or event, or perhaps a miracle that you observed which cannot be explained by any natural law or explanation.

Praying Scripture

ALMIGHTY AND WONDERFUL GOD, CREATOR OF ALL THINGS, I PRAISE YOU. I THANK YOU THAT YOU CAN MAKE SOMETHING OUT OF NOTHING, THAT YOU BRING LIFE WHERE THERE IS ONLY DEATH. THANK YOU, GOD, THAT YOU SAVED ME THROUGH THE SACRIFICE OF YOUR SON, JESUS CHRIST, ON THE CROSS AT CALVARY. AMEN.

Further Reflection

Day 2   Leviticus 20:26
Day 3   Malachi 2:10
Day 4   Hebrews 2:7
Day 5   Psalm 8:6-8
Day 6   Psalm 33:13-15
Day 7   2 Corinthians 4: 6, 7, 16

Week 3

The Phythagoreans (530 B. C.)

Phythagoras, a great philosopher and mathematician started the first "organized religion." The Phythagoreans adhered to a sort of moral code that anticipated the ethic codes of later religions (e.g., Hammurabi's Code and the Ten Commandments). His ethics, admittedly seem facile and nugatory by modern standards. The Phythagorean Brotherhood, for instance, was not allowed to eat beans. Phythagoras, however, was the first philosopher to require some standard of behavior from his followers. One can imagine what a novel and important step this was–that a religion would require a commitment from its adherents.

Furthermore, believing that the universe was composed of mathematical formulas and geometric shapes, Phythagoras formed the first "scientific religion" whose followers believed that reality was ordered by natural, immutable laws. The degree to which people understood these laws, determined their ability to control their fate.

> Phythagoras was the first philosopher to require some standard of behavior from his followers. One can imagine what a novel and important step this was–that a religion would require a commitment from its adherents.

Passage

And again from another starting-point, Pythagoras, son of Muesarchos, a Samian, who was the first to call this matter by the name of philosophy, assumed as first principles the numbers an the symmetries existing in them, which he calls harmonies, and the elements compounded of both, that are called geometrical. And again he includes the monad and the undefined dyad among the first principles; and for him one of the first principles tends toward the creative and form-giving cause, which is intelligence, that is god, and the other tends toward the passive and material cause, which is the visible universe. And he says that the starting-point of number is the decade; for all Greeks and all barbarians count as far as ten, and when they get as far as this they return to the monad. And again, he says, the power of the ten is in the four and the tetrad. And the reason is this: if anyone returning from the monad adds the numbers in a series as far as the four, he will fill out the number ten (i.e. $1 + 2 + 3 + 4 \ 10$); but if he

goes beyond the number of the tetrad, he will exceed the ten
(*Pythagoras and the Pythagoreans: Passages in the Doxographists*).

Biblical Response

God does indeed require a response from His people. In fact, He
explicitly states what he expects in the inspired Word of God.

James 1: 22-25 Do not merely listen to the word, and so
deceive yourselves. Do what it says. Anyone who listens to the
word but does not do what it says is like a man who looks at his
face in a mirror and, after looking at himself, goes away and
immediately forgets what he looks like. But the man who looks
intently into the perfect law that gives freedom, and continues to
do this, not forgetting what he has heard, but doing it--he will be
blessed in what he does.

Journal Writing

Is it possible to have a good, moral, religion without the intentional
submission to a higher authority or power?

Praying Scripture

HELP ME, GOD, NOT MERELY TO LISTEN TO THE WORD,
BUT HELP ME TO BE A DOER OF THE WORD TOO. HELP ME
TO REMEMBER AND TO OBEY THE WORD OF GOD THAT
HAS BEEN SO FAITHFULLY PRESENTED TO ME. IN JESUS
NAME. AMEN.

Further Reflection

Day 2   1 John 2:4
Day 3   Deuteronomy 29: 18-19
Day 4   Job 15:31
Day 5   Psalm 20: 7-8
Day 6   Amos 6:1, 3, 13
Day 7   Galatians 6:7-8

Week 4

The Eleatic School (500 B.C.)

Perhaps no pre-Socratic philosophical movement had as much influence on Western thought than that of the Eleatic School. Its main proponent, Parmenides, argued that reality was indivisible and endless. There was no beginning or ending to time either. All things were the same. From the beginning of time, everything existed that was to exist and that which existed changed in form, but not in substance. Thus, change was impossible. Something might change in form–ice to water to steam–but it was the same in substance. Also, once a thing moved in one direction it continued to move in that direction until time and circumstances stopped it. This viewpoint, carried to its logical conclusion, had a profound effect on Western thought. For one thing, the

> The Eleatic School argued that reality was indivisible and endless.

whole Theory of Relativity proposed by Albert Einstein was based on a similar theory. Likewise, philosophers like David Hume, in his rejection of the miraculous, espoused an Eleatic view of reality.

Passage

(An imaginary conversation between Socrates and Parmenides)

"And would you make an idea of man apart from us and from all other human creatures, or of fire and water?" Socrates says. "I am often undecided, Parmenides, as to whether I ought to include them or not."

"And would you feel equally undecided, Socrates, about things of which the mention may provoke a smile? I mean such things as hair, mud, dirt, or anything else which is vile and paltry; would you suppose that each of these has an idea distinct from the actual objects with which we come into contact, or not?"

"Certainly not," said Socrates, "visible things like these are such as they appear to us, and I am afraid that there would be an absurdity in assuming any idea of them, although I sometimes get disturbed, and begin to think that there is nothing without an idea; but then again, when I have taken up this position, I run away, because I am afraid that I may fall into a bottomless pit of nonsense, and perish; and so I return to the ideas of which I was just now speaking, and occupy myself with them."

"Yes, Socrates," said Parmenides, " that is because you are still young; the time will come, if I am not mistaken, when philosophy will have a firmer grasp of you, and then you will not despise even the meanest things; at your age, you are too much disposed to regard opinions of men. But I should like to know whether you mean that there are certain ideas of which all other things partake, and from which they derive their names; that similars, for example, become similar, because they partake of similarity; and great things become great, because they partake of greatness; and that just and beautiful things become just and beautiful, because they partake of justice and beauty? Then each individual partakes either of the whole of the idea or else of a part of the idea? Can there be any other mode of participation?"

"There cannot be," Socrates said. "Then do you think that the whole idea is one, and yet, being one, is in each one of the many? Why not, Parmenides? Because one and the same thing will exist as a whole at the same time in many separate individuals, and will therefore be in a state of separation from itself" (*Parmenides*, by Plato).

Biblical Response

In fact the world is complete because God made it that way; however, God miraculously intervenes to change history. He is not controlled by any natural law. A case in point: the miracle of salvation. This is truly a moment outside human history.

Peter 1:18-23 For you know that it was not with perishable things such as silver or gold that you were redeemed from the empty way of life handed down to you from your forefathers, but with the precious blood of Christ, a lamb without blemish or defect. He was chosen before the creation of the world, but was revealed in these last times for your sake. Through him you believe in God, who raised him from the dead and glorified him, and so your faith and hope are in God. Now that you have purified yourselves by obeying the truth so that you have sincere love for your brothers, love one another deeply, from the heart. For you have been born again, not of perishable seed, but of imperishable, through the living and enduring word of God.

Journal Writing
Recall an incident when God clearly intervened through circumstances or other means to protect, help, or bless you.

Praying Scripture
FATHER, GOD. THANK YOU THAT YOU CAN DO ALL THINGS, THAT YOU ARE ABLE TO SAVE EVEN ME. I THANK YOU THAT I AM BORN AGAIN, NOT OF PERISHABLE SEED, BUT OF IMPERISHABLE SEED, THROUGH THE LIVING AND ENDURING WORD OF GOD. AMEN.

Further Reflection
Day 2   Psalm 46:4
Day 3   1 Chronicles 16:35
Day 4   Psalm 107:9
Day 5   Isaiah 1:18
Day 6   Matthew 1:21
Day 7   Galatians 1:4

Week 5

The Pluralists (500 B.C.)

Philosophers Empedocles and Anaxagoras developed a philosophy that sought to replace the Ionian assumption of a single primary substance with four irreducible elements: air, water, earth, and fire. These four were alternately torn apart and brought together again by love and strife. The marriage of the physical and ethical universe is intriguing and was later developed by Plato. With no outside force in place, by chance the universe evolved from chaos to structure, and vice versa, in an eternal cycle. This whole process was so impressive that Empedocles regarded the eternal cycle as the proper object of religious worship. But that was not all. Anaxagoras, born 2400 years before Charles Darwin, developed a

> With no outside force in place, by chance the universe evolved from chaos to structure, and vice versa, in an eternal cycle.

theory of cosmic evolution. He argued that everything was made of infinitely small particles that combined and separated randomly. These combinations, however, predicted an unstoppable movement from chaos to structure. His theory ultimately led to the development of an atomic theory of matter.

Passage

Other things include a portion of everything, but mind is infinite and self-powerful and mixed with nothing, but it exists alone itself by itself. For if it were not by itself, but were mixed with anything else, it would include parts of all things, if it were mixed with any thing; for a portion of everything exists in everything, as has been said by me before, and things mingled with it would prevent it from having power over anything in the same way that it does now that it is alone by itself. For it is the most rarefied of all things and the purest, and it has all knowledge in regard to everything and the greatest power; over all that has life, both greater and less, mind rules. And mind ruled the rotation of the whole, so that it set it in rotation in the beginning. First it began the rotation from a small beginning, then more and more was included in the motion, and yet more will be included. Both the mixed and the separated and distinct, all things mind recognized. And whatever things were to be, and whatever things were, as many as are now, and whatever things shall be, all these mind arranged in order; and it arranged that rotation, according to which now rotate stars and sun and moon and air and aether, now that they are separated. Rotation itself caused the separation, and the dense is separated from the rare, the warm from the cold, the bright from the dark, the dry from the moist. And there are many portions of many things. Nothing is absolutely separated nor distinct, one thing from another, except mind. All mind is of like character, both the greater and the smaller. But nothing different is like anything else, but in whatever object there are the most, each single object is and was most distinctly these things (Anaxagoras).

Biblical Response

While the world is made of several hundred different basic elements, in fact each individual and thing is entirely unique. No two organisms are exactly alike.

Genesis 1: 24-25 And God said, "Let the land produce living creatures according to their kinds: livestock, creatures that move along the ground, and wild animals, each according to its kind." And it was so. God made the wild animals according to their kinds, the livestock according to their kinds, and all the creatures that move along the ground according to their kinds. And God saw that it was good.

Journal Writing

Describe a person whom is much different from you and write a prayer to God about him or her.

Praying Scripture

FATHER, GOD. THANK YOU THAT YOU CREATED THE HEAVEN AND THE EARTH, THAT YOU FILLED THAT EARTH WITH UNIQUE CREATURES, SOME SO COMPLICATED THAT THEY SURPASS HUMAN UNDERSTANDING. AND THEN YOU PRONOUNCED THAT IT WAS GOOD! THANK YOU, GOD, FOR ALLOWING ME TO BE A PART OF THIS WONDERFUL WORLD. AMEN.

Further Reflection

Week 6

The Sophists (500 B. C.)

Perhaps the most modern of Greek philosophers were the Sophists. Brilliant but wishwashy philosophers, the Sophists were pragmatists who sold their rhetorical services to a growing number of uneducated merchants. Like later Pragmatists, the Sophists grounded their reality in human experience, not in rationality or any other moral paradigm. For a price, they sold their ample rhetorical skills to the growing number of prosperous, but uneducated merchants. These merchants were the backbone of the new Greek city-states. The Sophists justifiably gained a reputation for being superficial, insincere, and pedantic. Sophists were not bothered at all. Rather, in their view, the end justified the means. Protagoras, the most famous Sophist, held that individuals had the right to judge all matters for themselves. Protagoras and his Sophist colleagues even denied the existence of an objective reality. Ethical rules needed to be followed only when it was to one's practical advantage to do so. Goodness, morality, and ethics were a reflection of culture rather than vice versa.

> Sophists were the first to deny the existence of an objective reality. Ethical rules needed to be followed only when it was to one's practical advantage to do so. Goodness, morality, and ethics were a reflection of culture rather than vice versa.

Passage

Education and admonition commence in the first years of childhood, and last to the very end of life. And if he obeys, well and good; if not, he is straightened by threats and blows, like a piece of bent or warped wood. At a later stage they send him to teachers, and enjoin them to see to his manners even more than to his reading and music; and the teachers do as they are desired. And when the boy has learned his letters and is beginning to understand what is written, as before he understood only what was spoken, they put into his hands the works of great poets, which he reads sitting on a bench at school; in these are contained many admonitions, and many tales, and praises, and encomia of ancient famous men, which he is required to learn by heart, in order that he may imitate or emulate them and desire to become like them. Then, again, the teachers of the lyre take similar care that their young disciple is temperate and gets into no mischief; and when they have taught him the use of the lyre, they introduce him to the poems of other excellent poets, who are the lyric poets; and these they set to music, and make their harmonies and rhythms quite familiar to the children's souls, in order that they may learn to be more gentle, and harmonious, and rhythmical, and so more fitted for speech and action; for the life of man in every part has need of harmony and rhythm. Then they send them to the master of gymnastics, in order that their bodies may better minister to the virtuous mind, and that they may not be compelled through bodily weakness to play the coward in war or on any other occasion. This is what is done by those who have the means, and those who have the means are the rich; their children begin to go to school soonest and leave off latest. When they have done with masters, the state again compels them to learn the laws, and live after the pattern which they furnish, and not after their own fancies; and just as in learning to write, the writing-master first draws lines with a style for the use of the young beginner, and gives him the tablet and makes him follow the lines, so the city draws the laws, which were the invention of good lawgivers living in the olden time; these are given to the young man, in order to guide him in his conduct whether he is commanding or obeying; and he who transgresses them is to be corrected, or, in other words, called to account, which is a term used not only in your country, but also in many others, seeing that justice calls men to account. Now when there is all this care about virtue private and public, why, Socrates, do you still wonder and doubt whether virtue can be taught? Cease to wonder, for the opposite would be far more surprising (Plato, *Protagoras*).

Biblical Response

At the heart of Sophism is the notion that God, if He exists at all, is insignificant because He is not involved in the affairs of mankind. The fact is, though, God is intimately involved with mankind and He has spoken clearly about that involvement.

> **John 3: 16** For God so loved the world that he gave his one and only Son, that whoever believes in him shall not perish but have eternal life.

Journal Writing

Describe an incident which at the time appeared to be so bad that God could not have been a part of it. Then, you discovered the "bad thing" was the best thing for all concerned.

Praying Scripture

ABBA, FATHER, THANK YOU THAT YOU ARE SO INVOLVED IN HUMAN AFFAIRS THAT YOU SENT YOUR SON TO DIE FOR OUR SINS. AMEN.

Further Reflection

Day 2   Isaiah 45:9
Day 3   Romans 9:20-21
Day 4   Psalm 57:7
Day 5   2 Thesssalonians 3:3
Day 6   Revelation 22:11
Day 7   Psalm 108:1

Week 7

Socrates (469-399 B. C.)

Socrates was one of the most influential but mysterious figures in Western philosophy. He wrote nothing, yet he had a profound influence on someone who did: Plato. Plato carefully recorded most of his dialogues. Unlike earlier philosophers, Socrates' main concern was with ethics. There was nothing remotely pragmatic about Socrates who was the consummate idealist. Until his day, philosophers invested most of their time explaining the natural world. In fact, the natural world often intruded into the abstract world of ideas and reality. Socrates kept both worlds completely separate. To Socrates, the natural laws governing the rotation of the earth were merely uninteresting speculation of no earthly good. Socrates was more interested in such meaty concepts as "virtue" and "justice." Taking issue with the Sophists, Socrates believed that ethics, specifically virtue, must be learned and practiced like any trade. One was not born virtuous; one developed virtue as he would a good habit. It could be practiced only by experts. There was, then, nothing pragmatic about the pursuit of virtue. It was systematic; it was intentional. Virtue was acquired and maintained by open and free dialogue. For the first time, the importance of human language was advanced by a philosopher (to reappear at the end of the 20th century in Post-modern philosophy).

> For the first time, the importance of human language was advanced by a philosopher.

Passage

I would have you look to yourselves; that is a service which you may always be doing to me and mine as well as to yourselves. And you need not make professions; for if you take no thought for yourselves, and walk not according to the precepts which I have given you, now for the first time, the warmth of your professions will be of no avail (Socrates speaking in Plato, *Phaedo*).

Biblical Response

Ecclesiastes 1:13-15 What a heavy burden God has laid on men! I have seen all the things that are done under the sun; all of them are meaningless, a chasing after the wind. What is twisted cannot be straightened; what is lacking cannot be counted.

Journal Writing

Describe the wisest person you know. Include his or her strengths, weaknesses, and other pertinent chararacteristics.

Praying Scripture

GOD, WE RECOGNIZE THAT HUMAN WISDOM IS FOLLY. WE UNDERSTAND THAT TRUE, ABIDING, AND LIFE-CHANGING TRUTH ONLY COMES BY READING AND UNDERSTANDING THE WORD OF GOD. WE ALSO KNOW THAT YOU ALONE ARE THE AUTHOR OF OUR FAITH. AMEN.

Further Reflection

Day 2   Philippians 3:12-15
Day 3   Colossians 2:9-11
Day 4   Colossians 3:14
Day 5   Psalm 18:32
Day 6   Proverbs 2:21
Day 7   Deuteronomy 5:32

Week 8

Plato (Born 428 B. C.)

There was no more important philosopher in Western culture than Socrates' disciple, Plato. Plato, like Socrates, regarded ethics as the highest branch of knowledge. Plato stressed the intellectual basis of virtue, identifying virtue with wisdom. Plato believed that the world was made of *forms* (such as, a rock) and *ideas* (such as, virtue). The ability of human beings to appreciate forms made a person

> Plato stressed the intellectual basis of virtue, identifying virtue with wisdom.

virtuous. Knowledge came from the gods; opinion was from man. Virtuous activity, then, was dependent upon knowledge of the forms.

Passage

And now, I said, let me show in a figure how far our nature is enlightened or unenlightened: Behold! Human beings living in a underground den, which has a mouth open towards the light and reaching all along the den; here they have been from their childhood, and have their legs and necks chained so that they cannot move, and can only see before them, being prevented by the chains from turning round their heads. Above and behind them a fire is blazing at a distance, and between the fire and the prisoners there is a raised way; and you will see, if you look, a low wall built along the way, like the screen which marionette players have in front of them, over which they show the puppets.

     I see.

     And do you see, I said, men passing along the wall carrying all sorts of vessels, and statues and figures of animals made of wood and stone and various materials, which appear over the wall? Some of them are talking, others silent.

     You have shown me a strange image, and they are strange prisoners.

Like ourselves, I replied; and they see only their own shadows, or the shadows of one another, which the fire throws on the opposite wall of the cave?

     True, he said; how could they see anything but the shadows if they were never allowed to move their heads?

     And of the objects which are being carried in like manner

they would only see the shadows? (Plato, "The Allegory of the Cave," *The Republic*)

Biblical Response

> **John 8: 12** When Jesus spoke again to the people, he said, "I am the light of the world. Whoever follows me will never walk in darkness, but will have the light of life."

Journal Writing

Write your testimony–your personal experience of your decision to follow Jesus and the results of that decision.

Praying Scripture

GOD OF LIGHT, GOD OF LIFE, WE THANK YOU THAT OUR LORD, YOUR SON, JESUS CHRIST, IS THE LIGHT OF THE WORLD. WE THANK YOU THAT WHOEVER FOLLOWS HIM WILL NEVER WALK IN DARKNESS, BUT WILL HAVE THE LIGHT OF LIFE. AMEN.

Further Reflection

Day 2   Psalm 27:1
Day 3   Psalm 119:105
Day 4   Isaiah 58:8
Day 5   Isaiah 60:19-20
Day 6   John 3:19-21
Day 7   John 9:5

Week 9

Plato (cont.)

The most famous concept of Plato's work was the concept of "love." "Love" to Plato was a "form" from which virtue flowed. Compare and contrast this view of love with a view from a man trained in the teachings of Plato: the Apostle Paul.

> "Love" to Plato was a "form" from which virtue flowed.

Passage

"First Chaos came, and then broad-
  bosomed Earth,
  The everlasting seat of all that is,
  And Love."

In other words, after Chaos, the Earth and Love, these two, came into being. Also Parmenides sings of Generation:
  "First in the train of gods, he fashioned Love."

The veriest coward would become an inspired hero, equal to the bravest, at such a time; Love would inspire him. That courage which, as Homer says, the god breathes into the souls of some heroes, Love of his own nature infuses into the lover. . . .And greatly as the gods honour the virtue of love, still the return of love on the part of the beloved to the lover is more admired and valued and rewarded by them, for the lover is more divine; because he is inspired by God. Now Achilleus was quite aware, for he had been told by his mother, that he might avoid death and return home, and live to a good old age, if he abstained from slaying Hektor. Nevertheless he gave his life to revenge his friend, and dared to die, not only in his defense, but after he was dead. Wherefore the gods honoured him even above Alcestis, and sent him to the Islands of the Blest. These are my reasons for affirming that Love is the eldest and noblest and mightiest of the gods, and the chiefest author and giver of virtue in life, and of happiness after death (Plato's *Symposium*).

Biblical Response

1 Cor. 13 Love is patient, love is kind. It does not envy, it does not boast, it is not proud. It is not rude, it is not self-seeking, it is not easily angered, it keeps no record of wrongs. Love does not delight in evil but rejoices with the truth. It always protects, always trusts, always hopes, always perseveres.

Love never fails. But where there are prophecies, they will cease; where there are tongues, they will be stilled; where there is knowledge, it will pass away. For we know in part and we prophesy in part, but when perfection comes, the imperfect disappears. When I was a child, I talked like a child, I thought like a child, I reasoned like a child. When I became a man, I put childish ways behind me. Now we see but a poor reflection as in a mirror; then we shall see face to face. Now I know in part; then I shall know fully, even as I am fully known.

And now these three remain: faith, hope and love. But the greatest of these is love.

Journal Writing

Love can be the strongest emotion in human experience. What is the difference between agape Υεϒ;Ω love and eros Ω ℧, love? Have you experienced agape love?

Praying Scripture

GOD OF LOVE, GOD OF LIGHT, GOD OF HOPE, I THANK YOU THAT YOU HAVE UNCONDITIONAL LOVE TOWARD YOUR CHILDREN. I THANK YOU THAT YOUR LOVE NEVER FAILS, THAT YOUR LOVE IS PERFECT. PLEASE HELP ME TO LOVE OTHERS AS YOU LOVE ME. AMEN.

Further Reflection

Day 2   John 17:26
Day 3   John 17:23
Day 4   Deuteronomy 10:12
Day 5   Deuteronomy 7:9
Day 6   2 John 6
Day 7   Jude 21

Week 10

Aristotle (Born 350 B. C.)

To Plato, knowledge and virtue were inseparable. To Aristotle, they were unconnected. Aristotle was not on a search for absolute truth. He was not even certain it existed. Truth, beauty, and goodness were to be observed and quantified from human behavior and the senses but they were not the legal tender of the land. Goodness in particular was not an absolute and in Aristotle's opinion it was much abused. Goodness was an average between two absolutes. Aristotle said that mankind should strike a balance between passion and temperance, between extremes of all sorts. He said that good people should seek the "Golden Mean" defined as a course of life that was never extreme. Finally, while Plato argued that reality lay in knowledge of the gods, Aristotle argued that reality lay in empirical, measurable knowledge. To Aristotle, reality was tied to purpose and to action. For these reasons, Aristotle, became known as the father of modern science.

> Aristotle was the first agnostic.

Passage

Good seems different in different actions and arts; it is different in medicine, in strategy, and in the other arts likewise. What then is the good of each? Surely that for whose sake everything else is done. In medicine this is health, in strategy victory, in architecture a house, in any other sphere something else, and in every action and pursuit the end; for it is for the sake of this that all men do whatever else they do. Therefore, if there is an end for all that we do, this will be the good achievable by action, and if there are more than one, these will be the goods achievable by action. So the argument has by a different course reached the same point; but we must try to state this even more clearly. Since there are evidently more than one end, and we choose some of these (e.g. wealth, flutes, and in general instruments) for the sake of something else, clearly not all ends are final ends; but the chief good is evidently something final. Therefore, if there is only one final end, this will be what we are seeking, and if there are more than one, the most final of these will be what we are. (Aristotle, *Nicomachean Ethics*).

Biblical Response

The fact is, everyone is without goodness. There is no "Golden Mean."

Romans 3: 12 All have turned away, they have together become worthless; there is no one who does good, not even one.

Journal Writing

Describe something good that Jesus has done through a Christian you know.

Praying Scripture

GOD OF JUDGEMENT, GOD OF MERCY, WE CONFESS THAT WE ARE NOT GOOD. WE BRING NOTHING TO YOU BUT OUR SIN AND UNRIGHTEOUSNESS. HOWEVER, WE THANK YOU, FATHER, THAT THROUGH OUR ACCEPTANCE OF THE SACRIFICE OF JESUS CHRIST ON THE CROSS, WE ARE SAVED. AMEN.

Further Reflection

Day 2   Psalm 120: 2, 5-7
Day 3   Proverbs 8:13
Day 4   Amos 3:2-3
Day 5   Hebrews 12:14
Day 6   Proverbs 10:23
Day 7   James 5:16

Week 11

Aristotle (cont.)

Aristotle's most enduring impact occurred in the area of metaphysics--philosophical speculation about the nature, substance, and structure of reality. It is not physics--concerned with the visible or natural world. Metaphysics is concerned with explaining the non-physical world. Aristotle, then advanced the discussion about God, the human soul, and the nature of space and time. What makes this particularly interesting is Aristotle's penchant for delving into the metaphysical by talking about the gods in human terms. Aristotle said, "All men by nature desire to know" and it is by the senses that the gods were known--or not. Faith had nothing to do with it. In other words, Aristotle, for the first time, discussed the gods as if they were quantified entities. He spoke about them as if they were not present. The Hebrews had done this earlier (Genesis 3) but Aristotle was probably not aware of Moses' text. While some Christian thinkers such as Augustine and Aquinas employed Aristotelian logic in their discussions about God, they never speculated about His existence as Aristotle did. They only used Aristotle's techniques to understand more about Him.

> Aristotle, for the first time discussed the gods as if they were quantified entities. He spoke about them as if they were not present.

Passage

All men by nature desire to know. An indication of this is the delight we take in our senses; for even apart from their usefulness they are loved for themselves; and above all others the sense of sight. For not only with a view to action, but even when we are not going to do anything, we prefer seeing (one might say) to everything else. The reason is that this, most of all the senses, makes us know and brings to light many differences between things. By nature animals are born with the faculty of sensation, and from sensation memory is produced in some of them, though not in others. And therefore the former are more intelligent and apt at learning than those which cannot remember; those which are incapable of hearing sounds are intelligent though they cannot be taught, e.g. the bee, and any other race of animals that may be like it; and those which besides memory have this sense of hearing can be taught. The animals other than man live by appearances and memories, and have but little of connected experience; but the human race lives also by art and reasonings. Now from memory experience is produced in men; for the several memories of the same thing produce finally the capacity for a single experience (Aristotle, *Metaphysics*).

Biblical Response

Even before Aristotle discussed God as if He did not exist, Adam and Eve did the same thing at the dawn of history.

> **Genesis 3:1-3** Now the serpent was more crafty than any of the wild animals the Lord God had made. He said to the woman, "Did God really say, 'You must not eat from any tree in the garden'?" The woman said to the serpent, "We may eat fruit from the trees in the garden, but God did say, 'You must not eat fruit from the tree that is in the middle of the garden, and you must not touch it, or you will die.' "

Journal Writing

What is your favorite Scripture? Why?

Praying Scripture

GOD, FORGIVE ME WHEN I LIVE MY LIFE AS IF YOU ARE NOT ALIVE AND PRESENT. WHAT FOOLS WE ARE TO LIVE OUR LIVES AS IF YOU DO NOT SEE WHAT WE DO! AS IF THERE ARE NO CONSEQUENCES FOR MY ACTIONS! FORGIVE ME AND HELP ME TO REMEMBER ALWAYS THAT YOU ARE OMNIPRESENT AND OMNISCIENT. HELP ME TO BE TRULY THANKFUL THAT YOU LOVE ME AND SENT YOUR SON TO DIE FOR ME. AMEN.

Further Reflection

Week 12

Cynicism (350 B. C.)

Inevitably prosperity brings a philosophical price tag: cynicism. Cynics are often ultra-conservatives who yearn for the "good old days" when thinkers were less impressionable in their demeanor. Such was the case in the Greek Enlightenment that saw the cynic Diogenes arise. For the first time, philosophers began to talk about the individual in earnest. Diogenes, a sort of 300 B. C. bohemian, dressed and lived in a counter-cultural fashion. He was weird! Whereas Socrates *talked* about living an *avant guard* lifestyle, Diogenes actually lived it. Diogenes argued that his Greek peers spent too much time pursuing material things that were at

> For the first time, philosophers began to talk about the individual in earnest, as if he were a subject to be studied.

best unnecessary for life and at worst a profound distraction. A story is told that Alexander the Great once approached Diogenes and asked him what he could do to reward Diogenes for his friendship. Diogenes, who happened to be relaxing in the sun, responded to the most powerful political figure in the world, "Stop blocking my sun."

Passage

One of the sayings of Diogenes was that most men were within a finger's breadth of being mad; for if a man walked with his middle finger pointing out, folks would think him mad, but not so if it were his forefinger. . . .All things are in common among friends. . . . Be of good cheer, I see land (Diogenes).

Biblical Response

Solomon answers the cynic.

> **Ecclesiastes 12: 6-8** Remember him--before the silver cord is severed, or the golden bowl is broken; before the pitcher is shattered at the spring, or the wheel broken at the well, and the dust returns to the ground it came from, and the spirit returns to God who gave it. "Meaningless! Meaningless!" says the Teacher. "Everything is meaningless!"

Journal Writing

Discuss a particularly discouraging, or difficult day, and how God turned it around.

Praying Scripture

LORD, I THANK YOU THAT YOU HAVE GIVEN MEANING TO MY LIFE. I WILL REMEMBER YOU--BEFORE THE SILVER CORD IS SEVERED, OR THE GOLDEN BOWL IS BROKEN; BEFORE THE PITCHER IS SHATTERED AT THE SPRING, OR THE WHEEL BROKEN AT THE WELL, AND THE DUST RETURNS TO THE GROUND IT CAME FROM, AND THE SPIRIT RETURNS TO GOD WHO GAVE IT. "MEANINGLESS! MEANINGLESS!" SAYS THE TEACHER. "EVERYTHING IS MEANINGLESS!" WHERE ELSE CAN I TURN FOR SALVATION? IN YOU, IN YOU ALONE, IS THERE HOPE, HAPPINESS, AND ETERNAL LIFE. AMEN.

Further Reflection

Day 2   John 7:38
Day 3   Luke 11:33-36
Day 4   John 11:25-26
Day 5   Philippians 4:6-7
Day 6   1 John1:9
Day 7   1 John 5:14

Week 13

Skepticism (300 B. C.)

Skepticism, like cynicism, was a reactionary philosophy. It was formulated by the Pyrrhonists, a school of Greek philosophy deriving its name from its founder, Pyrrho of Elis. Pyrrho, whose primary concern was ethics, maintained that human beings could know nothing of the real nature of things, and that consequently the wise person would give up trying to do so. This philosophy anticipates 21st century Absurdism.

> Pyrrho, whose primary concern was ethics, maintained that human beings could know nothing of the real nature of things, and that consequently the wise person would give up trying to do so.

Passage

He [Pyrrho] himself has left nothing in writing, but his pupil Timon says that whoever wants to be happy must consider these three questions: first, how are things by nature? Secondly, what attitude should we adopt towards them? Thirdly, what will be the outcome for those who have such an attitude? According to Timon, Pyrrho declared that things are equally indifferent, unmeasurable and inarbitrable. For this reason neither our sensations nor our opinions tell us truths or falsehoods. Therefore for this reason we should not put our trust in them one bit, but should be unopinionated, uncommitted and unwavering, saying concerning each individual thing that it no more is than is not, or both is and is not, or neither is nor is not (Eusebius, *Prep. Ev.* 14.18.2-5, Long & Sedley).

Biblical Response

There is a purpose to life and there are consequences for bad behavior. Regardless of what philosophers may write, God is the Creator of our lives, the Sovereign Lord of our destinies.

> **Romans 8: 28- 30** And we know that in all things God works for the good of those who love him, who have been called according to his purpose. For those God foreknew he also predestined to be conformed to the likeness of his Son, that he might be the firstborn among many brothers. And those he predestined, he also called; those he called, he also justified; those he justified, he also glorified.

Journal Writing

Recall an incident where you were punished for a bad choice. Discuss how God used it to make you a better person.

Praying Scripture

LORD, I KNOW THAT IN ALL THINGS GOD WORKS FOR THE GOOD OF THOSE WHO LOVE HIM, WHO HAVE BEEN CALLED ACCORDING TO HIS PURPOSE. I THANK YOU THAT YOU PREDESTINED TO BE CONFORMED TO THE LIKENESS OF YOUR SON. AND THOSE YOU PREDESTINED, YOU ALSO CALLED; THOSE YOU CALLED, YOU ALSO JUSTIFIED; THOSE YOU JUSTIFIED, YOU ALSO GLORIFIED. AMEN.

Further Reflection

Day 2   John 5:24
Day 3   John 10:27-29
Day 4   John 11:25-26
Day 5   Psalm 90:12
Day 6   Psalm 90:17
Day 7   Psalm 118:24

Week 14

Epicureanism (300 B.C.)

While Pyrrhic was writing, Epicurus was advocating an alternative doctrine. Epicurus was the Jerry Springer of his age. The aim of human life, he claimed, was to achieve maximum pleasure with the least effort and risk. Sound familiar? This philosophy became the bedrock of Post-modernism. Epicurus celebrated the individual's free will and desires. The subjective and personal were paramount. If it felt good, and hurt no one else, it was morally acceptable, even preferred, over any other alternative. Morality was tied to personal fulfillment rather than any external law, deity, or force. This philosophical position invited mankind to a place of selfishness that still is very much with us.

> The aim of human life, Epicurus claimed, was to achieve maximum pleasure with the least effort and risk.

Passage

If the things that produce the pleasures of profligate men really freed them from fears of the mind concerning celestial and atmospheric phenomena, the fear of death, and the fear of pain; if, further, they taught them to limit their desires, we should never have any fault to find with such persons, for they would then be filled with pleasures from every source and would never have pain of body or mind, which is what is bad. A blessed and indestructible being has no trouble himself and brings no trouble upon any other being; so he is free from anger and partiality, for all such things imply weakness. Death is nothing to us; for that which has been dissolved into its elements experiences no sensations, and that which has no sensation is nothing to us. The magnitude of pleasure reaches its limit in the removal of all pain. When such pleasure is present, so long as it is uninterrupted, there is no pain either of body or of mind or of both together (Epicurus).

Biblical Response

The fact is, suffering and pain are sometimes necessary and the ability to accept necessary pain is a sign of maturity.

> **Galatians 2 :20** I have been crucified with Christ and I no longer live, but Christ lives in me. The life I live in the body, I live by faith in the Son of God, who loved me and gave himself for me.

Journal Writing

Write about an example of selfish living which you have observed in today's world.

Praying Scripture

I HAVE BEEN CRUCIFIED WITH CHRIST AND I NO LONGER LIVE, BUT CHRIST, YOU LIVE IN ME. THE LIFE I LIVE IN THE BODY, I NOW LIVE BY FAITH IN YOU, WHO LOVED ME AND GAVE YOURSELF FOR ME. THANK YOU! AMEN.

Further Reflection

Day 2   Psalm 84:10-12
Day 3   Psalm 77:11-12
Day 4   Psalm 73:28
Day 5   Psalm 32:11
Day 6   Psalm 42:8
Day 7   Psalm 31:24

Week 15

Stoicism (300 B.C.)

Ably represented by Roman slave Epictetus and the Roman emperor Marcus Aurelius, Stoicism became the most influential school of the Greco-Roman world,. The Stoics taught that one can achieve happiness only by rejecting material comforts and by dedicating oneself to a life of reason and virtue. Human reason was also considered part of the divine Logos, and therefore immortal. Each person was part of God and all people form a universal family. Stoicism celebrated the human spirit, disciplined and sublime. It became the measuring rod against which all social and religious institutions were measured.

> Stoicism celebrated the human spirit and it became the measuring rod against which all social and religious institutions were measured.

Passage

Begin the morning by saying to thyself, I shall meet with the busybody, the ungrateful, arrogant, deceitful, envious, unsocial. All these things happen to them by reason of their ignorance of what is good and evil. But I who have seen the nature of the good that it is beautiful and of the bad that it is ugly, and the nature of him who does wrong, that it is akin to me, not [only] of the same blood or seed, but that it participates in [the same] intelligence and [the same] portion of the divinity, I can neither be injured by any of them, for no one can fix on me what is ugly, nor can I be angry with my kinsman, nor hate him. For we are made for co-operation, like feet, like hands, like eyelids, like the rows of the upper and lower teeth. To act against one another then is contrary to nature; and it is acting against one another to be vexed and to turn away. Though thou shouldest be going to live three thousand years, and as many times ten thousand years, still remember that no man loses any other life than this which he now lives, nor lives any other than this which he now loses. The longest and shortest are thus brought to the same. For the present is the same to all, though that which perishes is not the same: and so that which is lost appears to be a mere moment. For a man cannot lose either the past or the future: for what a man has not, how can any one take this from him? These two things then thou must bear in mind: the one, that all things from eternity are of like forms and come round in a circle, and that it makes no difference whether a man shall see the same things during a hundred years or two hundred, or an infinite time; and the second, that the longest liver and he who will die soonest lose just the same. For the present is the only thing of which a man can be deprived, if it is true that this is the only thing which he has, and that a man cannot lose a thing if he has it not (Marcus Aurelius, *Meditations*).

Biblical Response

The Stoics have much truth: life should be lived simply and completely. However, the thing that gives life meaning is following the Lord Jesus Christ. He alone makes life worthwhile.

Matthew 5:3-12
Blessed are the poor in spirit, for theirs is the kingdom of heaven.
Blessed are those who mourn, for they will be comforted.
Blessed are the meek, for they will inherit the earth.
Blessed are those who hunger and thirst for righteousness, for they will be filled.
Blessed are the merciful, for they will be shown mercy.
Blessed are the pure in heart, for they will see God.
Blessed are the peacemakers, for they will be called sons of God.
Blessed are those who are persecuted because of righteousness, for theirs is the kingdom of heaven.
Blessed are you when people insult you, persecute you and falsely say all kinds of evil against you because of me. Rejoice and be glad, because great is your reward in heaven, for in the same way they persecuted the prophets who were before you.

Journal Writing

Describe an ordinary, godly, spirit-filled person, whose name would never appear in the headlines, who nonetheless has changed the course of history.

Praying Scripture
LORD, I AM BLESSED BECAUSE YOU BLESS ME. THANK YOU. HELP ME TO LIVE A LIFE THAT MANIFESTS THE BEATITUDES. AMEN.

Further Reflection
Day 2   Matthew 10:29
Day 3   2 Corinthians 9:8-10
Day 4   Philippians 4:19
Day 5   1 Chronicles 17:27
Day 6   Matthew 6:11
Day 7   3 John 2

Week 16

Neoplatonism (A.D. 50)

Neoplatonism was both a revival of Platonic metaphysics and an effective competitor of Christianity. Central to Neoplatonism was phenomenology, or the study or description of subjects. Thus, an experience of ecstasy, in which one became one with God, was the source of all reality. For the first time, philosophy dared to cross the threshold from philosophy to experiential religion. The line between metaphysics and ethics had been crossed by the earlier Greek philosophers, but until now no one dared to speak of a religious experience as a philosophical phenomenon. In fact, the Neoplatonics defined what this religious experience was. With unabashed boldness the Neoplatonics argued that science and rationalism can and were the highest form of religious experience. This was the Star Wars religion of the thrd century A.D. The universe emanated from the Force, or Logos. It was layered according

> Neoplatonism dared to speak of a religious experience as a philosophical phenomenon

to stages of purity. The highest goal of life was to rid oneself of dependence on any corporal comfort. This bold but strange philosophy/religion invited its followers to experience a rationalistic theophany that came only to those who discarded humanity and embraced divinity. Neoplatonism evolved into Gnosticism, one of the most powerful heresies of the early church.

Passage

Pleasure and distress, fear and courage, desire and aversion, where have these affections and experiences their seat? Clearly, either in the Soul alone, or in the Soul as employing the body, or in some third entity deriving from both. And for this third entity, again, there are two possible modes: it might be either a blend or a distinct form due to the blending. And what applies to the affections applies also to whatsoever acts, physical or mental, spring from them. We have, therefore, to examine discursive-reason and the ordinary mental action upon objects of sense, and enquire whether these have the one seat with the affections and experiences, or perhaps sometimes the one seat, sometimes another. And we must consider also our acts of Intellection, their mode and their seat. And this very examining principle, which investigates and decides in these matters, must be brought to light (Plotinus, *The Six Anneads*).

Biblical Response

Neoplatonism, as strange and unappealing as it seems to us today, in fact was a powerful enemy of early Christianity. Its emphasis on hedonism and experience appealed to thousands of Romans. What does the Bible say about the Logos?

> **John 1: 1-3** In the beginning was the Word (υῶεῶ, Logos), and the Word was with God, and the Word was God. He was with God in the beginning. Through him all things were made; without him nothing was made that has been made.

Journal Writing

How does the believer know the difference between a genuine spiritual experience yet emotional and a false spiritual experience, manifesting itself in the garb of an emotional experience?

Praying Scripture

LORD, I THANK YOU THAT YOU ARE THE WORD. I KNOW THAT THROUGH YOU ALL THINGS WERE MADE. WITHOUT YOU NOTHING WAS MADE THAT HAS BEEN MADE. PLANT YOUR LOGOS, WORD, IN MY HEART. AMEN.

Further Reflection

Day 2   Hebrews 1:18   Maybe Heb 1:8 ?
Day 3   2 Timothy 2:15
Day 4   2 Peter 1:21
Day 5   1 Corinthians 2:12
Day 6   Hebrews 1:1-2
Day 7   Romans 1:4

Week 17

Augustine (A.D. 354-430)

It was never clear to Augustine where philosophy ended and theology began. For that reason alone Augustine was one of the most important theologians in world history. This man of God perhaps did more than any person to claim philosophy as a discipline for God.

Augustine argued that religious faith and philosophical understanding were complementary and that one must "believe in order to understand and understand in order to believe." Augustine spoke for a generation of believers at the end of the Roman empire. In Augustine, Plato's division of the world into the reality of True

> One must believe in order to understand and understand in order to believe.

Being as well as the separation of the soul from the body were given Christian interpretations. Augustine's "beatific vision of God" (*Confessions*, Book IV, Ch. 16) was very similar to Plato's "gazing upon the forms."

Passage

Though there are very many and great nations all over the earth, whose rites and customs, speech, arms, and dress, are distinguished by marked differences, yet there are no more than two kinds of human society, which we may justly call two cities, according to the language of our Scriptures. The one consists of those who wish to live after the flesh, the other of those who wish to live after the spirit. . . . Thus the things necessary for this mortal life are used by both kinds of men and families alike, but each has its own and widely different aim in using them. The earthly city, which does not live by faith, seeks an earthly peace, and the end it proposes, in the well-ordered concord of civil obedience and rule, is the combination of men's wills to attain the things which are helpful to this life. The heavenly city, or rather the part of it which sojourns on earth and lives by faith, makes use of this peace only because it must, until this mortal condition which necessitates it shall pass away (Augustine, *City of God*).

Biblical Response

Augustine understood that Christians are citizens of heaven, not of this earth. No matter what happens on earth, the believer is really a citizen of heaven.

> **Psalm 48: 1-2** Great is the Lord, and most worthy of praise, in the city of our God, his holy mountain. It is beautiful in its loftiness, the joy of the whole earth. Like the utmost heights of Zaphon is Mount Zion, the city of the Great King.

Journal Writing

Augustine's life was transformed by the power of the Holy Spirit but this was no doubt partly precipitated by the faithful prayers of his mother. Describe an instance in which God faithfully answered prayer in your life.

Praying Scripture

LORD, I AM NOT AFRAID OF THE TERROR BY NIGHT, OR THE ENEMY BY DAY. I WILL BE STRONG, BY YOUR GRACE, BECAUSE I AM MORE THAN A CONQUEROR THROUGH YOU. FOR I AM CONVINCED THAT NEITHER DEATH NOR LIFE, NEITHER ANGELS NOR DEMONS, NEITHER THE PRESENT NOR THE FUTURE, NOR ANY POWERS, NEITHER HEIGHT NOR DEPTH, NOR ANYTHING ELSE IN ALL CREATION, WILL BE ABLE TO SEPARATE US FROM THE LOVE OF GOD THAT IS IN CHRIST JESUS OUR LORD. AMEN.

Further Reflection

Day 2   Luke 18:1
Day 3   1 Timothy 2:8
Day 4   Ephesians 3:11-12
Day 5   Hebrews 4:16
Day 6   Jude 20
Day 7   Revelation 5:8

Week 18

Scholasticism (1100-1300)

In the 11th century a revival of philosophical thought began as a result of a group of mostly Christian thinkers, notably Thomas Aquinas. This movement, called Scholasticism, with varying degrees of success, attempted to use natural human reason--in particular, the philosophy and science of Aristotle--to understand the metaphysical content of Christian revelation. Scholasticism attempted a dangerous task which many judged to be a failure based on this premise: Christianity can never be a philosophy before it is a religion. Nonetheless, as Aquinas argued, the fact that God's knowledge is absolute

> Scholasticism, with varying degrees of success, attempted to use natural human reason--in particular, the philosophy and science of Aristotle--to understand the metaphysical content of Christian revelation.

does not mean that philosophical speculation, particularly Aristotelian speculation, is an automatic threat to Christian faith.

Passage

Just as God is not an existent according to this existence, but rather the nature of entity is eminently in Him, and so He is not in all ways devoid of entity; so even He is not in all ways devoid of knowledge that He may not be known. But He is not known by the mode of other existing things, which can be comprehended by the created intellect. Although God stands more distantly from every intelligible thing, according to the propriety of nature than the intelligible from the sensible, nevertheless, the notion of knowablity is more befitting to God (Thomas Aquinas).

Biblical Response

Aquinas knew well enough that God was the beginning and end of all knowledge. He merely posited that we could still employ our intellect.

> **Jeremiah 9: 23-24** This is what the Lord says: "Let not the wise man boast of his wisdom or the strong man boast of his strength or the rich man boast of his riches, but let him who boasts boast about this: that he understands and knows me, that I am the Lord, who exercises kindness, justice and righteousness on earth, for in these I delight," declares the Lord.

Journal Writing

The great Christian apologist G. K. Chesterton once lamented that contemporary century Christians do not know how to speak to unbelievers–the only thing we do well is speak to ourselves. Write down the names of your unsaved friends and purpose first to pray for them and then to speak to them about your faith.

Praying Scripture

LORD, I WILL NOT BOAST OF MY WISDOM OR MY STRENGTH OR MY RICHES, BUT I WILL BOAST ABOUT THIS: THAT YOU UNDERSTAND AND KNOW ME, THAT YOU ARE THE LORD WHO EXERCISES KINDNESS, JUSTICE AND RIGHTEOUSNESS ON EARTH. AMEN.

Further Reflection

Day 2   James 3:17
Day 3   1 John 2: 20, 27
Day 4   2 Timothy 1:7
Day 5   John 9:5, 39
Day 6   1 John 5:20
Day 7   Psalm 25:4-5

Week 19

Erasmus (1466-1536)

Everyone is familiar with the Renaissance, a time of artistic awakening in the 16th century. Erasmus was part of the Northern European Renaissance. A priest, a scientist, a genius, Erasmus made an indelible mark on his era. Perhaps the most enduring philosophical thought he advanced was his discussion about the self. Erasmus, for the first time, discussed things like happiness as being centered in the self or personhood of the man or woman. Happiness was based on some narcissist notions of self-love. While Erasmus did not create a system of psychology, he nonetheless started a discussion that would be revived in the works of Descartes and Freud.

> Erasmus, for the first time, discussed things like happiness as being centered in the self or personhood of the man or woman. Happiness was based on some narcissist notions of self-love.

Passage

Lastly, what is that in the whole business of a man's life he can do with any grace to himself or others --for it is not so much a thing of art, as the very life of every action, that it be done with a good mien -- unless this my friend and companion, Self-love, be present with it? Nor does she without cause supply me the place of a sister, since her whole endeavors are to act my part everywhere. For what is more foolish than for a man to study nothing else than how to please himself? To make himself the object of his own admiration? And yet, what is there that is either delightful or taking, nay rather what not the contrary, that a man does against the hair? Take away this salt of life, and the orator may even sit still with his action, the musician with all his division will be able to please no man, the player be hissed off the stage, the poet and all his Muses ridiculous, the painter with his art contemptible, and the physician with all his slip-slops go a-begging. Lastly, you will be taken for an ugly fellow instead of youthful, and a beast instead of a wise man, a child instead of eloquent, and instead of a well-bred man, a clown. So necessary a thing it is that everyone flatter himself and commend himself to himself before he can be commended by others Lastly, since it is the chief point of happiness "that a man is willing to be what he is," you have further abridged in this my Self-love, that no man is ashamed of his own face, no man of his own wit, no man of his own parentage, no man of his own house, no man of his manner of living, not any man of his own country; so that a Highlander has no desire to change with an Italian, a Thracian with an Athenian, not a Scythian for the Fortunate Islands. O the singular care of Nature, that in so great a variety of things has made all equal! Where she has been sometimes sparing of her gifts she has recompensed it with the mote of self-love; though here, I must confess, I speak foolishly, it being the greatest of all other her gifts: to say nothing that no great action was ever attempted without my motion, or art brought to perfection without my help (Erasmus, *In Praise of Folly*).

Biblical Response

Happiness is secondary to pleasing God; our real joy is in obeying Him. In this passage Nehemiah's community is happy for no other reason than that they have heard the Word of God.

> **Nehemiah 8: 10** Nehemiah said, "Go and enjoy choice food and sweet drinks, and send some to those who have nothing prepared. This day is sacred to our Lord. Do not grieve, for the joy of the Lord is your strength."

Journal Writing

Part of Christian maturity is accepting necessary suffering. Recall an incident where you had to endure discomfort or suffering for your faith. How did it feel? In what ways did it advance the purposes of Christ's Kingdom?

Praying Scripture

I THANK YOU, GOD, THAT YOU HAVE PROVIDED ME EVERYTHING I NEED. I CONSIDER IT A GREAT PLEASURE TO SERVE YOU. YOUR JOY IS MY STRENGTH. AMEN.

Further Reflection

Week 20

Michel de Montaigne (1533-1592)

Montaigne, a French nobleman, reintroduced Greek skepticism to Western culture. His skepticism, however, assumed a much more strident tone. "All that is certain is that nothing is certain" could easily have been written by 20th century Existentialists. Modern in substance and tone, Montaigne's writings redefined some of the parameters of 16th century philosophy.

Montaigne's phrase "suspend judgment" became the watchword for European intellectuals. He invited modern Europe to "suspend judgment" in its assessment of newly discovered civilizations in North America and Africa. Montaigne became the champion of later

> Montaigne reintroduced Greek skepticism to Western culture.

ideologues who embraced cultural neutrality and diversity. He was far ahead of his time.

Passage

The laws of conscience, which we pretend to be derived from nature, proceed from custom; every one, having an inward veneration for the opinions and manners approved and received among his own people, cannot, without very great reluctance, depart from them, nor apply himself to them without applause. In times past, when those of Crete would curse any one, they prayed the gods to engage him in some ill custom. But the principal effect of its power is, so to seize and ensnare us, that it is hardly in us to disengage ourselves from its gripe, or so to come to ourselves, as to consider of and to weigh the things it enjoins. To say the truth, by reason that we suck it in with our milk, and that the face of the world presents itself in this posture to our first sight, it seems as if we were born upon condition to follow on this track; and the common fancies that we find in repute everywhere about us, and infused into our minds with the seed of our fathers, appear to be the most universal and genuine: from whence it comes to pass, that whatever is off the hinges of custom, is believed to be also off the hinges of reason; how unreasonably, for the most part, God knows (Montaigne, *Essays*).

Biblical Response

Few people today believe that there is anything inherently superior about one group of people over another. Certainly we are all equal in God's sight. However, at the same time, we are all called to embrace biblical principles of morality. While no nation has a corner on the market of moral truth, the Kingdom of God certainly does.

Galatians 3: 26-28 You are all sons of God through faith in Christ Jesus, for all of you who were baptized into Christ have clothed yourselves with Christ. There is neither Jew nor Greek, slave nor free, male nor female, for you are all one in Christ Jesus.

Journal Writing

Have you ever been guilty of prejudice? Recall that incidence in writing, and if you have not already done so, seek God's forgiveness.

Praying Scripture

I THANK YOU, GOD, THAT WE WHO ARE SAVED ARE ALL SONS [AND DAUGHTERS] OF GOD THROUGH FAITH IN CHRIST JESUS, FOR ALL OF US WHO WERE BAPTIZED INTO CHRIST HAVE CLOTHED OURSELVES WITH CHRIST. THERE IS NEITHER JEW NOR GREEK, SLAVE NOR FREE, MALE NOR FEMALE, FOR WE ARE ALL ONE IN CHRIST JESUS. AMEN.

Further Reflection

Day 2   Philippians 2:5-7
Day 3   Mark 1:14-16
Day 4   Luke 6:19-21
Day 5   Romans 14:16-18
Day 6   Hebrews 12:27-29
Day 7   Revelation 1:5-7

Week 21

Francis Bacon (1561-1626)

Was Francis Bacon a Medieval man or a modern man? Bacon represented in broad relief the tensions of Elizabethan England. He was a scientist (most agree a "second-rate" scientist), a writer, and a philosopher. Philosophically, Bacon sought to purge the mind of what he called "idols," or a disposition to error. These came from human nature ("idols of the tribe"), from individual temperament and experience ("idols of the cave"), from language ("idols of the marketplace"), and from false philosophies ("idols of the theater"). Of earlier philosophers, he particularly criticized Aristotle. Within the writings of Plato, Bacon found a kindred spirit.

> Bacon advanced vigorously the idea that reasoning must triumph over theology.

Aristotle, with his propensity toward celebration of the human spirit over the power of the metaphysical, greatly offended Bacon. Nonetheless, Bacon advanced vigorously the idea that reasoning must triumph over theology. To Bacon knowledge, quite simply, was power. His greatest contribution to science was an insistence that inductive reasoning was a better form of reasoning than deductive reasoning.

Passage

An ant is a wise creature for itself, but it is a shrewd thing in an orchard or garden. And certainly men that are great lovers of themselves waste the public. Divide with reason between self-love and society; and be so true to thyself, as thou be not false to others; specially to thy king and country. It is a poor center of a mans actions, himself. It is right earth. For that only stands fast upon his own centre; whereas all things that have affinity with the heavens move upon the centre of another, which they benefit. The referring of all to a man's self is more tolerable in a sovereign prince; because themselves are not only themselves but their good and evil is at the peril of the public fortune. But it is a desperate evil in a servant to a prince, or a citizen in a republic. For whatsoever affairs pass such a mans hands, he crooketh them to his own ends; which must needs be often eccentric to the ends of his master or state. Therefore let princes, or states, choose such servants as have not this mark; except they mean their service should be made but the accessory. That which maketh the effect more pernicious is that all proportion is lost. It was disproportion enough for the servants good to be preferred before the masters; but yet it is a greater extreme, when a little good of the servant shall carry things against a great good of the masters. And yet that is the case of bad officers, treasurers, ambassadors, generals, and other false and corrupt servants; who set a bias upon their bowl, of their own petty ends and envies, to the overthrow of their masters great and important affairs. And for the most part, the good such servants receive is after the model of their own fortune; but the hurt they sell for that good is after the model of their masters fortune. And certainly it is the nature of extreme self-lovers, as they will set an house on fire, and it were but to roast their eggs; and yet these men many times hold credit with their masters, because their study is but to please them and profit themselves; and for either respect they will abandon the good of their affairs. Wisdom for a man's self is, in many branches thereof, a depraved thing. It is the wisdom of rats, that will be sure to leave a house somewhat before it fall. It is the wisdom of the fox, that thrusts out the badger, who digged and made room for him. It is the wisdom of crocodiles, that shed tears when they could devour. But that which is specially to be noted is, that those which (as Cicero says of Pompey) are *sui amantes, sine rivali* [lovers of themselves without a rival] are many times unfortunate. And whereas they have all their times sacrificed to themselves, they become in the end themselves sacrifices to the inconstancy of fortune, whose wings they sought by their self-wisdom to have pinioned (Bacon, *Essays*).

Biblical Response

1 Corinthians 1: 18- 21 For the message of the cross is foolishness to those who are perishing, but to us who are being saved it is the power of God. For it is written: "I will destroy the wisdom of the wise; the intelligence of the intelligent I will frustrate." Where is the wise man? Where is the scholar? Where is the philosopher of this age? Has not God made foolish the wisdom of the world? For since in the wisdom of God the world through its wisdom did not know him, God was pleased through the foolishness of what was preached to save those who believe.

Journal Writing
Describe an incident where you appeared foolish for the sake of the Gospel.

Praying Scripture
SURELY, FATHER GOD, IN TH AGE OF UNBELIEF, I AM A FOOLISH ONE.   THE MESSAGE OF THE CROSS IS TO ME THE POWER OF GOD. HELP ME IN MY ACTIONS AND IN MY WORDS TO BE FAITHFUL TO WITNESS TO THE CRUCIFIED CHRIST. AMEN.

Further Reflection
Day 2   Galatians 6:13-15
Day 3   Colossians 1:19-21
Day 4   Colossians 2:13-16
Day 5   Matthew 10:37-39
Day 6   Luke 14:26-28
Day 7   Ephesians 2:15-17

Week 22

Thomas Hobbes   (1588-1679)

Only Friederich Nietzsche was more pessimistic and prophetic in his message than Hobbes. Hobbes accurately predicted the nihilism that would be so endemic to the modern era. Hobbes was one of the first modern Western thinkers to provide a secular justification for political power. The philosophy of Hobbes marked a departure in Western philosophy from the religious emphasis of Scholasticism. Hobbes argued that people can either live under the violent, evil power of human nature or accept a state that has absolute power, in other words, a totalitarian state. There was no alternative.

> Hobbes was one of the first modern Western thinkers to provide a secular justification for political power.

Passage

Nature, the art whereby God hath made and governs the world, is by the art, of man, as in many other things, so in this also imitated, that it can make an artificial animal. For seeing life is but a motion of limbs, the beginning whereof is in some principal part within; why may we not say, that all *automata* (engines that move themselves by springs and wheels as doth a watch) have an artificial life? For what is the *heart* but a *spring* and the *nerves* but so many *strings* and the *joints* but so many *wheels*, giving motion to the whole body, such as was intended by the artificer? *Art* goes yet further, imitating that rational and most excellent work of nature, *man*. For by art is created that great *Leviathan* called a *Commonwealth* or *State*, in Latin *civitas,* which is but an artificial man, though of greater stature and strength than the natural, for whose protection and defense it was intended; and in which the *sovereignty* is an artificial *soul*, as giving life and motion to the whole body; the *magistrates* and other *officers* of judicature and execution, artificial *joints; reward* and *punishment*, by which fastened to the seat of the sovereignty every joint and member is moved to perform his duty, are the *nerves*, that do the same in the body natural; the *wealth* and riches of all the particular members are the *strength*; *salus populi,* the *people*s safety, its *business;counselors*, by whom all things needful for it to know are suggested unto it, are the *memory*; *equity* and *laws*, an artificial *reason* and *will*; *concord, health*;

sedition, *sickness*; and *civil war*, *death*. Lastly, the *pacts* and *covenants*, by which the parts of this body politic were at first made, set together, and united, resemble that *fiat,* or the *let us make man*, pronounced by God in the creation (Thomas Hobbes, *Leviathan*).

Biblical Response

The notion that unsaved people are inherently evil is biblical. However, the notion that equally evil men–even in a civil government–should have absolute power is without merit. Only God deserves to have absolute power.

Revelation 4: 10-11 The twenty-four elders fall down before him who sits on the throne, and worship him who lives for ever and ever. They lay their crowns before the throne and say: "You are worthy, our Lord and God, to receive glory and honor and power, for you created all things, and by your will they were created and have their being."

Journal Writing

If you are a male, are you willing to serve your country if drafted? Explain your reason. If you are a female, consider the same issue for your brother, spouse, father, or male cousin.

Praying Scripture

TO THE ONE WHO SITS ON THE THRONE, I PRAISE YOU. I WORSHIP YOU WHO LIVES FOR EVER AND EVER. I LAY MY CROWN BEFORE THE THRONE AND SAY: "YOU ARE WORTHY, OUR LORD AND GOD, TO RECEIVE GLORY AND HONOR AND POWER, FOR YOU CREATED ALL THINGS, AND BY YOUR WILL I WAS CREATED AND HAVE MY BEING." AMEN.

Further Reflection

Week 23

Rene Descartes   (1596-1650)

Descartes applied the rational inductive methods of mathematics, to philosophy. Before his time, philosophy had been dominated by the method of comparing and contrasting the views of recognized authorities. Rejecting this method, Descartes held nothing true until it seemed true to him. This phrase summarized his views,"I think, therefore I am." After Descartes, mankind replaced God as the center of the universe in the midst of many. This was an ominous moment in Western culture.

> After Descartes, mankind replaced God as the center of the universe in the midst of many. This was an ominous moment in Western culture.

Passage

But how do I know that there is not something different altogether from the objects I have now enumerated, of which it is impossible to entertain the slightest doubt? Is there not a God, or some being, by whatever name I may designate him, who causes these thoughts to arise in my mind ? But why suppose such a being, for it may be I myself am capable of producing them? Am I, then, at least not something? But I before denied that I possessed senses or a body; I hesitate, however, for what follows from that? Am I so dependent on the body and the senses that without these I cannot exist? But I had the persuasion that there was absolutely nothing in the world, that there was no sky and no earth, neither minds nor bodies; was I not, therefore, at the same time, persuaded that I did not exist? Far from it; I assuredly existed, since I was persuaded. But there is I know not what being, who is possessed at once of the highest power and the deepest cunning, who is constantly employing all his ingenuity in deceiving me. Doubtless, then, I exist, since I am deceived; and, let him deceive me as he may, he can never bring it about that I am nothing, so long as I shall be conscious that I am something. So that it must, in fine, be maintained, all things being maturely and carefully considered, that this proposition (pronunciatum) *I am, I exist*, is necessarily true each time it is expressed by me, or conceived in my mind (Descartes, *Meditation II*).

Biblical Response

"Being" is not as big a deal as we would like to think. We are men and women created by a Sovereign God. We exist because he created us. Period.

Hebrews 2: 6-8 For somewhere in the Scriptures it says, "What is man that you should think of him, and the son of man that you should care for him? For a little while you made him lower than the angels, and you crowned him with glory and honor. You gave him authority over all things." Now when it says "all things," it means nothing is left out. But we have not yet seen all of this happen.

Journal Writing

What do you want to be when you grow up? Why?

Praying Scripture

GOD, OUR CREATOR AND REDEEMER. I AM, BECAUSE YOU ARE. I AM CREATED BY YOU AND YOU ALONE, HAVE THE RIGHT TO DETERMINE MY FUTURE. I THANK YOU, THEREFORE, THAT "I THINK AND I AM," ARE POSSIBLE ONLY BECAUSE YOU ARE THE GREAT "I AM' WHO GUIDES MY THINKING. AMEN.

Further Reflection

Day 2   2 Corinthians 5:9-10
Day 3   2 Corinthians 4:6-7
Day 4   2 Corinthians 5:6-8
Day 5   John 5:24
Day 6   John 6:37
Day 7   John 6:51

Week 24

Benedictus de Spinoza (1632-1677)

Spinoza, an intellectual child of the Enlightenment, attempted to develop an ethical system from the existential rationalism of Descartes. It will never happen! One does not pull a moral, ethical system from a rational hat. Spinoza, beginning with that thesis, went downhill. He argued that human morality arose from self-interest. Also, he argued that there was a sort of "commonality" and "community" that arose among men as we all sought our selfish ends. The concept "selfish community" is an oxymoron. In brief, Spinoza sought to discuss theological issues with philosophical terminology. It failed. It may have worked for Plato, who had never known the Living God of the Old and New Testaments, but it would never work for Spinoza, who knew the God of the Bible. And it would not work for later philosophers (e.g., David Hume).

> Spinoza argued that human morality arose from self-interest.

Passage

The perfection of things is to be reckoned only from their own nature and power; things are not more or less perfect, according as they delight or offend human senses, or according as they are serviceable or repugnant to mankind (Spinoza).

Biblical Response

The quote from Spinoza implies that there is no evil, that evil is merely a matter of opinion. Of course this is utter nonsense. In His Word, God is precise about what is evil and what is good.

Exodus 20: 1-17 And God spoke all these words: "I am the Lord your God, who brought you out of Egypt, out of the land of slavery. You shall have no other gods before me. You shall not make for yourself an idol in the form of anything in heaven above or on the earth beneath or in the waters below. You shall not bow down to them or worship them; for I, the Lord your God, am a jealous God, punishing the children for the sin of the fathers to the third and fourth generation of those who hate me, but showing love to a thousand {generations} of those who love me and keep my commandments. You shall not misuse the name of the Lord your God, for the Lord will not hold anyone guiltless who misuses his name. Remember the Sabbath day by keeping it holy. Six days you shall labor and do all your work, but the seventh day is a Sabbath to the Lord your God. On it you shall not do any work, neither you, nor your son or daughter, nor your manservant or maidservant, nor your animals, nor the alien within your gates. For in six days the Lord made the heavens and the earth, the sea, and all that is in them, but he rested on the seventh day. Therefore the Lord blessed the Sabbath day and made it holy. Honor your father and your mother, so that you may live long in the land the Lord your God is giving you. You shall not murder. You shall not commit adultery. You shall not steal. You shall not give false testimony against your neighbor. You shall not covet your neighbor's house. You shall not covet your neighbor's wife, or his manservant or maidservant, his ox or donkey, or anything that belongs to your neighbor.

Journal Writing
What are the consequences of disobeying God's laws?

Praying Scripture
LORD, I THANK YOU THAT I AM NOT MY OWN HIGHEST AUTHORITY. I THANK YOU THAT GOOD SHALL PREVAIL OVER EVIL. HELP ME, GOD, TO OBEY ALL YOUR COMMANDMENTS. AMEN.

Further Reflection

Day 2   Romans 5:18-20
Day 3   Romans 6:15-17
Day 4   Hebrews 4:10-12
Day 5   1 Peter 1:1-3
Day 6   1 John 2:5-7
Day 7   Hebrews 5:7-9

Week 25

John Locke (1632-1704)

Locke believed in reasoning and common sense, rather than in metaphysics. He regarded the mind of a person at birth as a *tabula rasa*--a blank slate upon which experience imprinted knowledge--and did not believe in the subjective. Locke believed in unalienable rights, rights that were given by God or another absolute power and were not given by government. If government did not give these

> Locke believed in reasoning and common sense, rather than in metaphysics.

rights, then it could not take them away. Inherent in Lockian thought was the notion that people were bascially good. It followed, then, since people were basically good, the best government was government that governed the least.

Passage

If severity carried to the highest pitch does prevail, and works a cure upon the present unruly distemper, it often brings in the room of it a worse and more dangerous disease, by breaking the mind; and then, in the place of a disorderly young fellow, you have a low spirited moped creature, who, however with his unnatural sobriety he may please silly people, who commend tame inactive children, because they make no noise, nor give them any trouble; yet at last, will probably prove as uncomfortable a thing to his friends, as he will be all his life an useless thing to himself and others. Beating them, and all other sorts of slavish and corporal punishments, are not the discipline fit to be used in the education of those we would have wise, good, and ingenuous men; and therefore very rarely to be applied, and that only in great occasions, and cases of extremity. On the other side, to flatter children by rewards of things that are pleasant to them, is as carefully to be avoided. He that will give to his son apples or sugar-plums, or what else of this kind he is most delighted with, to make him learn his book, does but authorize his love of pleasure, and cocker up that dangerous propensity, which he ought by all means to subdue and stifle in him. You can never hope to teach him to master it, whilst you compound for the check you gave his inclination in one place, by the satisfaction you propose to it in another. To make a good, a wise, and a virtuous man, 'tis fit he should learn to cross his appetite, and deny his inclination to riches, finery, or pleasing his palate, &c. whenever his reason advises the contrary, and his duty requires it. But when you draw him to do any thing that is fit by the offer of money, or reward the pains of learning his book by the pleasure of a luscious morsel; when you promise him a lace-cravat or a fine new suit, upon performance of some of his little tasks; what do you by proposing these as rewards, but allow them to be the good things he should aim at, and thereby encourage his longing for 'em, and accustom him to place his happiness in them? Thus people, to prevail with children to be industrious about their grammar, dancing, or some other such matter, of no great moment to the happiness or usefulness of their lives, by misapplied rewards and punishments, sacrifice their virtue, invert the order of their education, and teach them luxury, pride, or covetousness. For in this way, flattering those wrong inclinations which they should restrain and suppress, they lay the foundations of those future vices, which cannot be avoided but by curbing our desires and accustoming them early to submit to reason (John Locke, *Some Thoughts Concerning Education*).

Biblical Response

The fact is that mankind is by nature, evil. Only when we commit our lives to Christ are we redeemed. At that point, we are transformed from condemned sinners to new creatures who can defeat sin through dependence on the Lord.

> **Isaiah 59: 1-3** Surely the arm of the LORD is not too short to save, nor his ear too dull to hear. But your iniquities have separated you from your God; your sins have hidden his face from you, so that he will not hear. For your hands are stained with blood,
> your fingers with guilt. Your lips have spoken lies, and your tongue mutters wicked things.

Journal Writing

At baptism believers are named, affirmed, and blessed. If you have been baptized, recall your baptism experience or the day you confirmed your baptism vows, and explain what impact it had on your life.

Praying Scripture

FATHER, SURELY YOUR ARM IS NOT TOO SHORT TO SAVE,
NOR YOUR EAR TOO DULL TO HEAR. BUT MY INIQUITIES
HAVE SEPARATED ME FROM YOU. HOWEVER, THANKS TO
THE SACRIFICE OF CHRIST ON CALVARY, MY SINS ARE
FORGIVEN. THANK YOU! AMEN.

Further Reflection

Day 2   Romans 3:23-25
Day 3   1 Corinthians 1:29-31
Day 4   Romans 8:22-24
Day 5   Ephesians 1:13-15
Day 6   Ephesians 1:6-8
Day 7   Hebrews 9:11-13

Week 26

G. W. Leibniz (1646-1716)

To Leibniz, the universe was composed of countless, distinct conscious centers of spiritual force. Some existed in the human community; some existed with God. While Leibniz believed in God, he also believed that God created a world separate from His sovereignty. In other words, God was present, but if man wished to progress in his world he needed to invest more time in understanding the world and less time understanding God. Leibniz's views were quite Aristotelian. He was referenced by later Deists and Naturalists who compared the world to a watch. God wound the watch, but then walked away. God was alive but simply not active in His world. The theological notion that a powerful God stood around doing nothing while good and bad fought it out was a novel idea that had a depressing effect on all who believed it.

> Leibniz believed in a God who created a world separate from His sovereignty.

Passage

Truths of reason are necessary and their opposite is impossible: truths of fact are contingent and their opposite is possible (Leibniz).

Biblical Response

The notion that God is present in the world but chooses to be uninvolved in the world is troubling. It is one thing to say that He does not exist; it is quite another to say He is present but not active in human affairs. The Bible is clear that God is very present, very concerned, and very active in human affairs.

> **Psalm 139: 7-10** Where can I go from your Spirit? Where can I flee from your presence? If I go up to the heavens, you are there; if I make my bed in the depths, you are there. If I rise on the wings of the dawn, if I settle on the far side of the sea, even there your hand will guide me, your right hand will hold me fast. If I say, "Surely the darkness will hide me and the light become night around me," even the darkness will not be dark to you; the night will shine like the day, for darkness is as light to you.

Journal Writing

Describe a time when God pursued you when you after disobeyed Him and His Word. How did you know He was pursuing you? Did you send someone to encourage you in obedience? Did He engineer circumstances so that your sin was revealed?

Praying Scripture

GOD, WHERE CAN I GO FROM YOUR SPIRIT? WHERE CAN I FLEE FROM YOUR PRESENCE? IF I GO UP TO THE HEAVENS, YOU ARE THERE; IF I MAKE MY BED IN THE DEPTHS, YOU ARE THERE. IF I RISE ON THE WINGS OF THE DAWN, IF I SETTLE ON THE FAR SIDE OF THE SEA, EVEN THERE YOUR HAND WILL GUIDE ME, YOUR RIGHT HAND WILL HOLD ME FAST. IF I SAY, "SURELY THE DARKNESS WILL HIDE ME AND THE LIGHT BECOME NIGHT AROUND ME," EVEN THE DARKNESS WILL NOT BE DARK TO YOU; THE NIGHT WILL SHINE LIKE THE DAY, FOR DARKNESS IS AS LIGHT TO YOU. I PRAISE AND THANK YOU THAT YOU LOVE ME AND THAT YOU ARE PRESENT EVERYWHERE ALL THE TIME. I WILL REST IN YOUR SOVEREIGN GRACE. AMEN.

Further Reflection

Day 2   1 Corinthians 11:31-33
Day 3   2 Timothy 1:6-8
Day 4   Hebrews 12:6-11
Day 5   Revelation 3:18-20
Day 6   Titus 1:7-9
Day 7   Hebrews 12:1-2

Week 27

George Berkeley (1685-1753)

George Berkeley was the founder of Idealism. He held that neither matter nor truth existed independent of the mind. The heart and mind were the tour guides to reality. In fact, to Berkeley, reality was separate from everything that could be quantified. Berkeley revered subjectivity. Subjectivity was the oil that greased the wheels of life. In fact, subjectivity, or what Berkeley

> Berkeley called "intuition," was the voice of God to mankind.

called "intuition," was the voice of God to mankind. The intuition was part of the divine intervention in mankind's destiny. God spoke through the conscience and intuition, not through the mind. God certainly did not speak to mankind through any external witness, such as the Bible. Berkeley used two fictional characters, Hylas and Philonous to make his point. Hylas represented the view of normal common sense. Philonous represented Berkeley's views. In summary, reality to Berkeley existed and was accessed in the mind; there was no reality, in fact, outside the mind. This view evolved into the Pantheism of Romanticism and Transcendentalism.

Passage

Hyl. You were represented, in last night's conversation, as one who maintained the most extravagant opinion that ever entered into the mind of man, to wit, that there is no such thing as material substance in the world.

Phil. That there is no such thing as what philosophers call material substance, I am seriously persuaded: but, if I were made to see anything absurd or skeptical in this, I should then have the same reason to renounce this that I imagine I have now to reject the contrary opinion. *Hyl.* What I can anything be more fantastical, more repugnant to Common Sense, or a more manifest piece of Scepticism, than to believe there is no such thing as matter?

Phil. Softly, good Hylas. What if it should prove that you, who hold there is, are, by virtue of that opinion, a greater sceptic, and maintain more paradoxes and repugnances to Common Sense, than I who believe no such thing?

Hyl. You may as soon persuade me, the part is greater than the whole, as that, in order to avoid absurdity and skepticism, I should ever be obliged to give up my opinion in this point (George Berkeley, *Three Dialogues Between Hylas and Philonous in Opposition to Sceptics and Atheists*).

Biblical Response

The mind certainly is powerful and important. In fact, to a Christian, it is more powerful than the body or matter. After all, an idea, however abstract, is a powerful entity. What is more powerful than love? However true this may be in the area of metaphysics, it is not true in ethics. Ethics and morality are not a matter of the mind or intuition–they are subject to the absolute, immutable Word of God. A believer regards obedience to God's Word as more important how he "feels" or what he "thinks." That is the reality of things.

Hebrews 4: 12-13 For the word of God is living and active. Sharper than any double--edged sword, it penetrates even to dividing soul and spirit, joints and marrow; it judges the thoughts and attitudes of the heart. Nothing in all creation is hidden from God's sight. Everything is uncovered and laid bare before the eyes of him to whom we must give account.

Journal Writing

Give an example from your experience in which the Word of God changed your perspective on an important issue.

Praying Scripture

GOD, I THANK YOU THAT YOUR WORD IS LIVING AND ACTIVE. SHARPER THAN ANY DOUBLE-EDGED SWORD, IT PENETRATES EVEN TO DIVIDING SOUL AND SPIRIT, JOINTS AND MARROW; IT JUDGES THE THOUGHTS AND ATTITUDES OF THE HEART. NOTHING IN ALL CREATION IS HIDDEN FROM YOUR SIGHT. EVERYTHING IS UNCOVERED AND LAID BARE BEFORE YOUR EYES AND WE ARE ACCOUNTABLE TO YOU. AMEN.

Further Reflection

Week 28

David Hume (1711-1776)

Probably no philosopher disturbs this writer more than David Hume (except Nietzsche). Hume, for the first time in Western history, seriously suggested that there was no necessary connection between cause and effect. If there is no necessary effect from any necessary cause, how can there be a God, much less an omnipotent God? People, Hume argued, were captured by their senses. For better or worse all they had were their senses. Nothing else was real. There were no permanently necessary connections between different objects. Effects associated with particular causes were merely coincidental patterns of experience. Thus, with no predictable effect from a cause, there was no reason to fear any consequences resulting from any behavior, because there was no judgement. Morality was a wholly human construct governed by human needs and demands rather than by a higher authority (e.g., God). Hume opened the door to the modern world views of Naturalism and Realism.

> Hume, for the first time in Western history, seriously suggested that there was no necessary connection between cause and effect.

Passage

The plain consequence is (and it is a general maxim worthy of our attention), "that no testimony is sufficient to establish a miracle, unless the testimony be of such a kind, that its falsehood would be more miraculous, than the fact, which it endeavors to establish; and even in that case there is a mutual destruction of arguments, and the superior only gives us an assurance suitable to that degree of force, which remains, after deducting the inferior." When anyone tells me that he saw a dead man restored to life, I immediately consider with myself, whether it be more probable, that this person should either deceive or be deceived, or that the fact, which he relates, should really have happened. I weigh the one miracle against the other; and according to the superiority, which I discover, I pronounce my decision, and always reject the greater miracle. If the falsehood of his testimony would be more miraculous, than the event which he relates; then, and not till then, can he pretend to command my belief or opinion (David Hume, "Of Miracles" in *An Enquiry Concerning Human Understanding)*.

Biblical Response

However we feel about causes and effect, we do not break the laws of God; the laws of God break us. Bad choices have consequences.

> **Galatians 6:6-10** Do not be deceived: God cannot be mocked. A man reaps what he sows. The one who sows to please his sinful nature, from that nature will reap destruction; the one who sows to please the Spirit, from the Spirit will reap eternal life. Let us not become weary in doing good, for at the proper time we will reap a harvest if we do not give up. Therefore, as we have opportunity, let us do good to all people, especially to those who belong to the family of believers.

Journal Writing

Write about a choice you made which you knew contradicted God's Word, and the consequences you suffered because of that wrong choice. Next, describe a right choice you made and its effect on your life.

Praying Scripture

LORD, HELP ME NOT TO BECOME WEARY IN DOING GOOD, FOR AT THE PROPER TIME I WILL REAP A HARVEST IF I DO NOT GIVE UP. THEREFORE, AS I HAVE OPPORTUNITY, HELP ME TO DO GOOD TO ALL PEOPLE, ESPECIALLY TO THOSE WHO BELONG TO THE FAMILY OF BELIEVERS. AMEN.

Further Reflection

Day 2   Ephesians 4:7
Day 3   James 5:11
Day 4   2 Corinthians 7:9-11
Day 5   1 Peter 2:25
Day 6   Hosea 6:1
Day 7   Lamentations 3:40-41

Week 29

Immanuel Kant   (1724-1804)

From the "consequence-less" place of Hume to the subjectiveness of Kant was a small step. Whereas Descartes argued that there was knowledge that existed before experience (e.g., mathematics), and Hume argued that people could have experience separate from any knowledge, Kant now argued that reality was experience. But not everything was experience. Knowledge could not completely step away from experience, but there was some knowledge–called *a priori* knowledge–that could not be gained by experience. For example, Kant said that bachelors are unmarried. This was an *a priori* statement because the word

> Kant argued that reality was experience. If one could not experience something with his senses, then it was not real.

"bachelor" meant "unmarried male" whether the speaker meant this truth or the hearer experienced this truth. Truth, then, was limited to irreducible human-created structures. Morality and ethics would never be *a priori* truth. With only *a priori* knowledge Kant argued that morality was based on man's ability to act rationally, not on any *ipso facto* phenomenon.

Passage

Ancient Greek philosophy was divided into three sciences: Physics, Ethics, and Logic. This division is perfectly suitable to the nature of the thing, and the only improvement that can be made in it is to add the principle on which it is based, so that we may both satisfy ourselves of its completeness, and also be able to determine correctly the necessary subdivisions. All rational knowledge is either material or formal: the former considers some object, the latter is concerned only with the form of the understanding and of the reason itself, and with the universal laws of thought in general without distinction of its objects. Formal philosophy is called Logic. Material philosophy, however, which has to do with determinate objects and the laws to which they are subject, is again two-fold; for these laws are either laws of nature or of freedom. The science of the former is Physics, that of the latter, Ethics; they are also called natural philosophy and moral philosophy respectively. Logic cannot have any empirical part;

that is, a part in which the universal and necessary laws of thought should rest on grounds taken from experience; otherwise it would not be logic, i.e. a canon for the understanding or the reason, valid for all thought, and capable of demonstration. Natural and moral philosophy, on the contrary, can each have their empirical part, since the former has to determine the laws of nature as an object of experience; the latter the laws of the human will, so far as it is affected by nature: the former, however, being laws according to which everything does happen; the latter, laws according to which everything ought to happen. Ethics, however, must also consider the conditions under which what ought to happen frequently does not. We may call all philosophy empirical, so far as it is based on grounds of experience: on the other hand, that which delivers its doctrines from *à priori* principles alone we may call pure philosophy. When the latter is merely formal it is logic; if it is restricted to definite objects of the understanding it is metaphysics. In this way there arises the idea of a two-fold metaphysic--a metaphysic of nature and a metaphysic of morals. Physics will thus have an empirical and also a rational part. It is the same with Ethics; but here the empirical part might have the special name of practical anthropology, the name morality being appropriated to the rational part (Immanuel Kant, *Fundamental Principles of the Metaphysic of Morals*).

Biblical Response

Certainly no Christian wishes to act irrationally; however, the clear basis of morality is the Word of God, not rationality. As a point in fact, the moral and right thing to do may actually be irrational–as the following Scripture illustrates.

> **Matthew 5: 38-42** You have heard that it was said, 'Eye for eye, and tooth for tooth.' But I tell you, Do not resist an evil person. If someone strikes you on the right cheek, turn to him the other also. And if someone wants to sue you and take your tunic, let him have your cloak as well. If someone forces you to go one mile, go with him two miles. Give to the one who asks you, and do not turn away from the one who wants to borrow from you.

Journal Writing

Describe an incident in your life where the moral and right thing to do was irrational to the world but directly in line with the Word of God.

Praying Scripture

GOD, HELP ME TO OVERCOME EVIL WITH GOOD. HELP ME
TO OBEY YOUR WORDS, "IF SOMEONE STRIKES YOU ON
THE RIGHT CHEEK, TURN TO HIM THE OTHER ALSO. AND
IF SOMEONE WANTS TO SUE YOU AND TAKE YOUR TUNIC,
LET HIM HAVE YOUR CLOAK AS WELL. IF SOMEONE
FORCES YOU TO GO ONE MILE, GO WITH HIM TWO MILES.
GIVE TO THE ONE WHO ASKS YOU, AND DO NOT TURN
AWAY FROM THE ONE WHO WANTS TO BORROW FROM
YOU." LORD, IT IS HARD TO DO THESE THINGS, SO I'M
DEPENDING ON YOUR STRENGTH TO HELP ME OBEY YOU.
AMEN.

Further Reflection

Day 2   Psalm 26:12 — foot stands on level ground
Day 3   Psalm 27:1-6, 13
Day 4   Psalm 28: 6-8
Day 5   Psalm 145:4-7, 10-12
Day 6   Acts 5:31-32
Day 7   Psalm 89:1

Week 30

Jean Jacques Rousseau   (1712-1778)

Rousseau, the father of Romanticism, championed the idea that people were happiest in a "state of nature." To be in a "state of nature" meant that mankind was outside the structures, however efficacious they might be, of government and society. Rousseau advocated one of the first "back-to-nature movements." At the heart of Rousseau's philosophy was the notion that mankind is basically good. Civilization, authority, and other humans have corrupted mankind.

> Rousseau advocated one of the first "back-to-nature movements."

American proponents of Romanticism included Ralph Waldo Emerson and Edgar Allan Poe.

Passage

The philosophers, who have examined the foundations of society, have, every one of them, perceived the necessity of tracing it back to a state of nature, but not one of them has ever arrived there. Some of them have not scrupled to attribute to man in that state the ideas of justice and injustice, without troubling their heads to prove, that he really must have had such ideas, or even that such ideas were useful to him: others have spoken of the natural right of every man to keep what belongs to him, without letting us know what they meant by the word belong; others, without further ceremony ascribing to the strongest an authority over the weakest, have immediately struck out government, without thinking of the time requisite for men to form any notion of the things signified by the words authority and government. All of them, in fine, constantly harping on wants, avidity, oppression, desires and pride, have transferred to the state of nature ideas picked up in the bosom of society. In speaking of savages they described citizens. Nay, few of our own writers seem to have so much as doubted, that a state of nature did once actually exist; though it plainly appears by Sacred History, that even the first man, immediately furnished as he was by God himself with both instructions and precepts, never lived in that state, and that, if we give to the books of Moses that credit which every Christian philosopher ought to give to them, we must deny that, even before the deluge, such a state ever existed among men, unless they fell into it by some extraordinary event: a paradox very difficult to maintain, and altogether impossible to prove (Jean Jacques Rousseau, *On the Inequality among Mankind*).

Biblical Response

The Bible is clear that original sin is real, and a part of the human condition. If we want proof, we need only remember the Holocaust of the 1940s or the terrorism of September 11, 2001.

John 3: 19-20 This is the verdict: Light has come into the world, but men loved darkness instead of light because their deeds were evil. Everyone who does evil hates the light, and will not come into the light for fear that his deeds will be exposed. But whoever lives by the truth comes into the light, so that it may be seen plainly that what he has done has been done through God.

Journal Writing

Some historians argue that the most important scientific breakthrough of the 20th century was the killing and disposing of 10,000 persons a day at Auschwitz. While they share our horror, they argue that, scientifically speaking, it was harder technologically to commit this crime than it was to put someone on the moon. Tell why you agree or disagree.

Praying Scripture

LORD GOD, I THANK YOU FOR THE LIGHT. HELP ME TO WALK IN THE LIGHT. I OPEN MYSELF UP TO YOU AND ACCEPT YOUR LIGHT INTO MY LIFE. I HIDE NOTHING FROM YOU. AMEN.

Further Reflection

Day 2   Psalm 69:5
Day 3   Romans 3:23
Day 4   Romans 6:23
Day 5   John 1:12
Day 6   Titus 3:5
Day 7   2 Corinthians 5:21

Week 31

William Godwin   (1756-1836)

Godwin, opposing Locke, argued that mankind had no natural rights. The community was ubiquitous and always held precedence over individual rights. It was not, however, that Godwin wanted little government; he wanted no government. He was the father of anarchism. In Godwin's ideal community there was no need of law. If there was a dispute, the community at large would solve the case, individually. The notion that there were individual rights, or a codex of governing laws, was anathema to Godwin.

> The notion that there were individual rights, or a codex of governing laws, was anathema to Godwin.

Passage

The true object of moral and political disquisition, is pleasure or happiness. The primary, or earliest class of human pleasures, is the pleasures of the external senses. In addition to these, man is susceptible of certain secondary pleasures, as the pleasures of intellectual feeling, the pleasures of sympathy, and the pleasures of self-approbation. The secondary pleasures are probably more exquisite than the primary: Or, at least, the most desirable state of man, is that, in which he has access to these sources of pleasure, and is in possession of a happiness the most varied and uninterrupted. This state is a state of high civilization (William Godwin).

Biblical Response

Again, at the heart of Godwin's philosophy is the false notion that people are basically good. The fact is, without the radical intervention of God through the sacrifice of His Son Jesus Christ on the cross, no one could be "good." Governments, then, are necessary to limit and to control human behavior that, if left to its own devices, would choose a harmful path.

> **Psalm 58: 3** Even from birth the wicked go astray; from the womb they are wayward and speak lies. Their venom is like the venom of a snake, like that of a cobra that has stopped its ears, that will not heed the tune of the charmer, however skillful the enchanter may be.

Journal Writing
Compare yourself with a biblical character.

Praying Scripture
LORD GOD, I CONFESS THAT I HAVE BEEN SINFUL BY
NATURE AND BY CHOICE. HOWEVER, I THANK YOU THAT
THROUGH JESUS CHRIST I HAVE BEEN REDEEMED.   AMEN.

Further Reflection
Day 2   Lamentations 3:22-23
Day 3   Micah 7:7
Day 4   Malachi 4:2
Day 5   1 Corinthians 15:57
Day 6   Psalm 138:4-6
Day 7   Psalm 136:26

Week 32

Soren Kierkegaard   (1813-1855)

Kierkegaard was an enigma. On one hand, he advanced a fairly orthodox Christian position. On the other hand, he inadvertently encouraged one of the most harmful heresies of the 20th century: Existentialism. Existentialism maintained that systematic philosophy not only imposed a false perspective on human existence but that it also, by explaining life in terms of logical necessity, became a means of avoiding choice and responsibility. He very nearly put religion in the same category as philosophy. Human beings, Kierkegaard argued, were nothing more than a compilation of choices, good and bad.

> Kierkegaard explained life in terms of logical necessity, became a means of avoiding choice and responsibility.

Passage

Father in Heaven! Hold not our sins up against us, But hold us up against our sins, So that the thought of Thee Should not remind us Of what we have committed, But of what thou didst forgive; Not how we went astray, But how Thou didst save us! (Kierkegaard)

Biblical Response

Kierkegaard's shortcoming was that he emphasized free will at the expense of the sovereignty of God. Nonetheless, we make choices every day that affect our lives.

> **Deuteronomy 30: 19-20** This day I call heaven and earth as witnesses against you that I have set before you life and death, blessings and curses. Now choose life, so that you and your children may live and that you may love the Lord your God, listen to his voice, and hold fast to him. For the Lord is your life, and he will give you many years in the land he swore to give to your fathers, Abraham, Isaac and Jacob.

Journal Writing

Besides your salvation, what is the most important decision you will make in your life? Why?

Praying Scripture

FATHER IN HEAVEN, THIS DAY I CALL HEAVEN AND EARTH AS WITNESSES THAT I CHOOSE LIFE, SO THAT I AND MY CHILDREN MAY LIVE AND THAT WE MAY LOVE THE LORD OUR GOD, LISTEN TO HIS VOICE, AND HOLD FAST TO HIM. FOR THE LORD IS OUR LIFE, AND HE WILL GIVE US MANY YEARS IN THE LAND HE SWORE TO GIVE TO OUR FATHERS, ABRAHAM, ISAAC AND JACOB. AMEN.

Further Reflection

Day 2   2 Samuel 2:32-34 — *don't exist*
Day 3   Psalm 27:1
Day 4   1 Chronicles 16:8-12
Day 5   Psalm 7:17
Day 6   1 Chronicles 16:23-27
Day 7   2 Samuel 22:4

Week 33

G. W. F. Hegel   (1770-1831)

Hegel, a decidedly modern philosopher, vigorously attacked everything scientific. Hegel believed strongly in the dialectic and polarity. Truth had no application if there were not opposites warring for its reality. For instance, if there was no evil, there was no good. There could be no good in the universe if there was no evil in the same universe. From the struggle between these polarities, or in the dialectic, there emerged truth. Hegel began with a thesis (a position put forward for argument). Opposed to this was a contradictory statement or antithesis. Out of their opposition came a synthesis which embraced both. Since the truth lay only in the whole system, this first synthesis was not yet the truth of the matter, but became a new thesis, with its corresponding antithesis and synthesis. And so on. Truth, then, was not absolute and always open to interpretation. Truth lay in the "search" of the "system."

> Truth had no application if there were not opposites warring for its reality.

Passage

Spirit is self-contained existence. Now this is Freedom, exactly. For if I am dependent, my being is referred to something which I am not; I cannot exist independently of something external. I am free, on the contrary, when my existence depends on myself (Hegel).

Biblical Response

Fidelity to God demands that we are loyal to His Word.

Luke 12: 8-9 I tell you, whoever acknowledges me before men, the Son of Man will also acknowledge him before the angels of God. But he who disowns me before men will be disowned before the angels of God.

Journal Writing

A perfect example of Hegelian thought is the way Americans discuss homosexuality. The Bible is clear that homosexuality is an abomination. One side argues this position vigorously. Still another side argues that homosexuality is perfectly natural and acceptable. Another position, urging compromise, argues that homosexuality is morally acceptable as long as there are mitigating circumstances, such as that the two parties involved love each other and are faithful to one another. Hogwash! Homosexuality was sinful, is sinful, and always shall be sinful because the Bible says it is. Not that homosexuals should be persecuted; no, they should be loved, but they must be told the truth. Discuss other Hegelian arguments raging in your world.

Praying Scripture

GOD, HELP ME TO ACKNOWLEDGE YOU IN ALL PLACES, AT ALL TIMES, ALL THE REST OF MY LIFE. AMEN.

Further Reflection

Day 2   Psalm 71:15, 19
Day 3   Judges 5:11
Day 4   Ezra 9:15
Day 5   Job 36:3
Day 6   Psalm 5:8
Day 7   Psalm 7:9

Week 34

Karl Marx   (1818-1883)

A disciple of G. W. F. Hegel was Karl Marx.
Marx, the father of Communism, applied Hegelian
theory to society. The proletariat fought
the bourgeoisie and in this struggle the
proletariat was cleansed and prepared for
its ultimate call to rule. To the
deterministic, atheistic Marx, Christianity
was a fairy tale created to placate weak
people.

> Christianity was a
> fairy tale created to
> placate weak people.

Passage

The history of all hitherto existing society is the history of class
struggles. Freeman and slave, patrician and plebian, lord and serf,
guild-master and journeyman, in a word, oppressor and oppressed,
stood in constant opposition to one another, carried on an
uninterrupted, now hidden, now open fight, a fight that each time
ended, either in a revolutionary reconstitution of society at large, or in
the common ruin of the contending classes. In the earlier epochs of
history, we find almost everywhere a complicated arrangement of
society into various orders, a manifold gradation of social rank. In
ancient Rome we have patricians, knights, plebians, slaves; in the
Middle Ages, feudal lords, vassals, guild-masters, journeymen,
apprentices, serfs; in almost all of these classes, again, subordinate
gradations. The modern bourgeois society that has sprouted from the
ruins of feudal society has not done away with class antagonisms. It
has but established new classes, new conditions of oppression, new
forms of struggle in place of the old ones. Our epoch, the epoch of
the bourgeoisie, possesses, however, this distinct feature: it has
simplified class antagonisms. Society as a whole is more and more
splitting up into two great hostile camps, into two great classes
directly facing each other -- bourgeoisie and proletariat. From the
serfs of the Middle Ages sprang the chartered burghers of the earliest
towns. From these burgesses the first elements of the bourgeoisie
were developed. The discovery of America, the rounding of the Cape,
opened up fresh ground for the rising bourgeoisie. The East-Indian
and Chinese markets, the colonisation of America, trade with the
colonies, the increase in the means of exchange and in commodities
generally, gave to commerce, to navigation, to industry, an impulse
never before known, and thereby, to the revolutionary element in the
tottering feudal society, a rapid development (Marx).

Biblical Application

Isaiah 40: 28-31 Do you not know? Have you not heard? The Lord is the everlasting God, the Creator of the ends of the earth. He will not grow tired or weary, and his understanding no one can fathom. He gives strength to the weary and increases the power of the weak. Even youths grow tired and weary, and young men stumble and fall; but those who hope in the Lord will renew their strength. They will soar on wings like eagles; they will run and not grow weary, they will walk and not be faint.

Journal Writing

Give concrete reasons from your life experiences which prove that God exists.

Praying Scripture

LORD, YOU ARE THE EVERLASTING GOD, THE CREATOR OF THE ENDS OF THE EARTH. YOU WILL NOT GROW TIRED OR WEARY, AND YOUR UNDERSTANDING NO ONE CAN FATHOM. YOU GIVE STRENGTH TO THE WEARY AND INCREASES THE POWER OF THE WEAK. EVEN THOUGH I MAY GROW TIRED AND WEARY, AND MAY SOMETIMES STUMBLE AND FALL; MY HOPE IS IN YOU. PLEASE RENEW MY STRENGTH. LET MEL SOAR ON WINGS LIKE EAGLES! HELP ME TO RUN AND NOT GROW WEARY! AMEN.

Further Reflection

Day 2   Proverbs 14:19
Day 3   Proverbs 19:21
Day 4   Joel 2:21, 23, 26
Day 5   Hosea 2:8, 21, 22
Day 6   Daniel 6:20-22
Day 7   Ezekiel 36:9-11, 30, 36

Week 35

Pierre Joseph Proudhon   (1809-1865)

This anarchist revolutionary, strong on practice, weak on theory, believed that mankind was neither good naturally nor bad because of circumstances. Mankind, to Proudhon, was wrongly made–a dud, so to speak. It was not mankind's fault that it had so much trouble–it was God's fault for making him this way. Therefore, in Proudhon's words, mankind's "destiny is perpetually to re-create his ideal in himself." In other words, "sinner save yourself." Since mankind could rely on no outside source to ameliorate him, governments, religions, and any other external authority were superfluous.

> Proudon instituted the last serious philosophical attempt to undermine the human will as a determining factor in human decision-making.

Passage

Justice, as we can see from the example of children and savages, is the last and slowest to grow of all the faculties of the soul; it needs an energetic education in struggle in adversity (Proudhon).

Biblical Response

Human beings are far more valuable than Proudhon understood we are. We are created in the image of God. To reject human original sin is to reject the journey back to redemption and to violate the very nature of humanity.

> **Genesis 1: 26-28** Then God said, "Let us make man in our image, in our likeness, and let them rule over the fish of the sea and the birds of the air, over the livestock, over all the earth, and over all the creatures that move along the ground." So God created man in his own image, in the image of God he created him; male and female he created them. God blessed them and said to them, "Be fruitful and increase in number; fill the earth and subdue it. Rule over the fish of the sea and the birds of the air and over every living creature that moves on the ground."

Journal Writing

What are the inevitable results of a world view that rejects the concept that mankind is created in the image of God? Hint: Consider the unborn, elderly people, and mentally/ physically challenged people

Praying Scripture

LORD, THANK YOU THAT YOU HAVE CREATED ME IN YOUR IMAGE. HELP ME TO BE FAITHFUL TO THE CALLING THAT THIS PRESENTS TO ME. AMEN.

Further Reflection

Day 2   Job 31:15
Day 3   Psalm 8:5
Day 4   Psalm 100:3
Day 5   Psalm 119:73
Day 6   Psalm 139:14
Day 7   Isaiah 64:8

Week 36

Arthur Schopenhauer
(1788-1860)

Schopenhauer thought that Hegel's concept of dialectic (e.g., progress and insight comes through the struggle of ideals) was nonsense. The key to understanding Schopenhauer was understanding his concept of the will. The human will, with all its chauvinism and narcissism, was the most powerful human impulse. The will was a transcendent thing in itself, separate from all other entities. In fact, to Schopenhauer, it was what made *homo sapiens* uniquely human. The will to succeed, the will to overcome, the will to survive, and the will to persevere all determined our

> The human will, with all its chauvinism and narcissism, was the most powerful human impulse.

humanity. Anything for example, Christianity that took that will away (in his estimation) or weakened that will was false and harmful. Schopenauer preferred the more spiritually seductive religions of Buddhism and Hinduism. In fact, to Schopenhauer, by debilitating human will, the Christian God was the source of all evil and pain.

Passage

One such pretext and deceit is love. The will of the species masks itself under the pleasures of love with the purpose of perpetuating the desire for life in others. In so doing, it satisfies its own will to live. Another pretext and deceit is egoism, which impels us to increase the pains of others in the hope of gaining some advantage in our own miserable life. Still another deceit and illusion is progress which, in actuating itself, only makes more acute the sense of distress (Schopenhauer paraphrased).

Biblical Response

In his farewell address to His disciples, Jesus reminds them one final time of the importance of love and obedience. Love was, is, and always will be essential to Christian believers.

> **John 14: 16-21** Before long, the world will not see me anymore, but you will see me. Because I live, you also will live. On that day you will realize that I am in my Father, and you are in me, and I am in you. Whoever has my commands and obeys them, he is the one who loves me. He who loves me will be loved by my Father, and I too will love him and show myself to him.

Journal Writing

Using stories from your life, respond to Schopenhauer's concern that Christianity takes away our will to survive.

Praying Scripture

FATHER, I REALIZE THAT YOU ARE IN ME, AND I AM IN YOU. I HAVE JESUS' COMMANDS AND I OBEY THEM, SINCE I AM ONE WHO LOVES HIM. I LOVE JESUS AND WILL BE LOVED BY YOU, MY FATHER GOD. PLEASE REVEAL YOUR SON TO ME. AMEN.

Further Reflection

Day 2   1 Corinthians 2:11
Day 3   1 Corinthians 6:20
Day 4   Romans 7:14-25
Day 5   Job 9:4
Day 6   Psalm 104:24
Day 7   Amos 5:8

Week 37

Herbert Spencer (1820-1903)

Herbert Spencer took the Hegelian, Naturalistic, evolutionary biological views of Charles Darwin and applied it to human society. This English sociologist, in other words, argued that in biological sciences and in the social sciences, the fittest and the strongest survived. He argued that world societies were slowly evolving into their highest order. That evolution was manifested primarily from an inexorable movement from simple to complex. Spencer and other evolutionists, created theories that were tautologies. A tautology is a way of saying the same thing twice. Spencer argued in favor of natural selection, an obvious tautology. Natural selection was a theory that predicted that the fittest organisms will produce the most offspring, and it defined the fittest organism as the ones which produce the most offsprings. Finally, concerning the random creation of life, there are about 2000 enzymes and the chance of obtaining them all in a random trial is 1 part in 10 to the $40,000^{th}$ power, a ridiculously unlikely probability that could not be overcome even if the whole universe consisted of organic soup ready to hatch into life (Fred Hoyle). Which came first, the chicken or the egg? The only answer is "neither." God is the creator and designer of this universe and all its life. The flaws of Spencer's evolutionary reasoning are obvious.

> Spencer argued that in biological sciences and in the social sciences the fittest and the strongest survived.

Passage

The general principle must lead us to anticipate that the diverse forms of religious belief which have existed and which still exist, have all a basis in some ultimate fact. Judging by analogy the implication is, not that any one of them is altogether right, but that in each there is something right more or less disguised by other things wrong. It may be that the soul of truth contained in erroneous creeds is extremely unlike most, if not all, of its several embodiments; and indeed if, as we have good reason to assume, it is much more abstract than any of them, its unlikeness necessarily follows. But some essential verity must be looked for. To suppose that these multiform conceptions should be one and all absolutely groundless, discredits too profoundly that average human intelligence from which all our individual intelligences are inherited (Herbert Spencer, *First Principles*).

Biblical Response

If Spencer's principles were right, then God would have had no reason to destroy Noah's community. In fact, human society, like human beings, will become worse, not better, over time. Only through the powerful intervention of God through His Son Jesus Christ is there hope for positive change in human society and in human beings.

> **Genesis 6: 5-7** The Lord saw how great man's wickedness on the earth had become, and that every inclination of the thoughts of his heart was only evil all the time. The Lord was grieved that he had made man on the earth, and his heart was filled with pain. So the Lord said, "I will wipe mankind, whom I have created, from the face of the earth--men and animals, and creatures that move along the ground, and birds of the air--for I am grieved that I have made them."

Journal Writing

Christianity is diametrically opposed to evolution, on all points, at all levels. For example, the weak are not destroyed by natural selection: they are esteemed. The weak are not only important, they will inherit the Kingdom of God (Matt. 5). Give examples of this truth from your own experience.

Praying Scripture

LORD, FORGIVE ME FOR EMBRACING TRUTHS THAT I HAVE NOT JUDGED ACCORDING TO SCRIPTURE. FOR ONE THING, I AM TOO PROUD TO BE COUNTED AMONG THE MEEK, BUT I ASK THAT YOU HUMBLE ME SO THAT I CAN BE MORE LIKE YOU. ON DAYS WHERE I DOUBT AND WORRY, I AM VERY GLAD THAT YOU LOVE THE WEAK AND POOR. AMEN.

Further Reflection

Day 2   Acts 6:4
Day 3   Romans 1:9
Day 4   Romans 12:12
Day 5   Ephesians 1:15-16
Day 6   1 Thessalonians 5:17
Day 7   2 Timothy 1:3

Week 38

Friedrich Nietzsche   (1844-1890)

Nietzsche was more of a prophet than a philosopher.
Most of his hellish predictions about the modern
world have come true. British historian Paul Johnson, *Modern Times*,
wrote "Among the advanced races, the decline and ultimately the
collapse of the religious impulse would leave a huge vacuum. The
history of modern times is in great part the history of how that vacuum
is filled. Nietzsche rightly perceived that the most likely candidate
would be what he called the
'Will to Power,' which offered
a far more comprehensive
and in the end more plausible
explanation of human
behavior than either Marx or
Freud. In place of religious
belief, there would be secular
ideology. Those who once
filled the ranks of the
totalitarian clergy would
become totalitarian politicians. And, above all, the Will to Power
would produce a new kind of messiah, uninhibited by any religious
sanctions whatever, and with an unappeasable appetite for controlling
mankind. The end of the old order, with an unguided world adrift in a
relativistic universe, was a summons to such gangster-statesmen to
emerge. They were not slow to make their appearance." They
appeared in the persons of Adolf Hitler and Josef Stalin.

> Among the advanced races, the
> decline and ultimately the
> collapse of the religious impulse
> would leave a huge vacuum.
> The history of modern times is in
> great part the history of how that
> vacuum is filled.

Passage

What is good?--Whatever augments the feeling of power, the will to
power, power itself, in man. What is evil?--Whatever springs from
weakness. What is happiness?--The feeling that power increases--that
resistance is overcome. Not contentment, but more power; not peace
at any price, but war; not virtue, but efficiency (virtue in the
Renaissance sense, virtu, virtue free of moral acid). The weak and the
botched shall perish: first principle of our charity. And one should
help them to it (Friedrich Nietzsche, *The Anti-Christ*).

Biblical Response

God will not be mocked. The Book of Daniel contains the story of people mocking God. God is not amused. In the midst of the revelry, God visits transgressors with His Word.

> **Daniel 5: 25-28** This is the inscription that was written: Mene , Mene , Tekel , Parsin. This is what these words mean: Mene: God has numbered the days of your reign and brought it to an end. Tekel: You have been weighed on the scales and found wanting. Peres : Your kingdom is divided and given to the Medes and Persians.

Journal Writing

Read the newspaper, or even better, read *World* Magazine, and discuss who the "supermen" are. Who are the contemporary people who are defying the Living God?

Praying Scripture

LORD, THANK YOU THAT YOU SPEAK FORTHRIGHTLY AND PLAINLY TO ME THROUGH YOUR WORD. THANK YOU THAT YOU ARE IN ABSOLUTE CONTROL OF EVERYTHING. AMEN.

Further Reflection

Day 2   2 Timothy 2:3, 22
Day 3   2 Timothy 3:2-7
Day 4   Hosea 6:6
Day 5   Luke 4:8
Day 6   1 Timothy 2:8
Day 7   Revelation 15:4

Week 39

Martin Heidegger (1889-1976)

When I read Heidegger I don't know if he was incredibly brilliant or insane. To a large degree, however, the spirit of the 20th century is captured in Heidegger. Heidegger, like Nietzsche, discussed ultimate things. In fact, he answered the basic Western philosophical question: "What is it, to be?" The meaning of the world, to Heidegger, must be discovered outside the person–not in the person. There was no form or essence in a person that would help him make sense of the world. It was through language that man discovered and created his world. In fact, language was the world. When a man realized his condition he had a sense of fear or *angst*. As a man overcame this dread, he grew in strength.

> The meaning of the world, to Heidegger, must be discovered outside the person–not in the person.

Passage

The language machine regulates and adjusts in advance the mode of our possible usage of language through mechanical energies and functions. The language machine is-and above all, is still becoming-one way in which modern technology controls the mode and the world of language as such. Meanwhile, the impress is still maintained that man is the master of the language machine. But the truth of the matter might well be that the language machine takes language into its management and thus masters the essence of the human being (Heidegger).

Biblical Response

How sad it is that people look to their own strength and ingenuity for deliverance instead of looking to the God of the Universe, especially since He is always, everywhere available.

> **John 14: 6** Jesus answered, "I am the way and the truth and the life. No one comes to the Father except through me.

Journal Writing

Respond to this acquaintance who says, "I think people can reach God in many different ways. Christianity, Buddhism, Hinduism, Islam–they are all different roads to the same destination."

Praying Scripture

LORD, THANK YOU THAT YOU ARE THE WAY, THE TRUTH, AND THE LIFE. HELP ME TO WALK THAT WAY, KNOW THE TRUTH, AND LIVE THE LIFE FOR ALL THE REMAINDER OF MY DAYS. AMEN.

Further Reflection

Day 2   Psalm 150:1-6
Day 3   Psalm 69:5-6
Day 4   Philippians 4:8
Day 5   Exodus 33:13
Day 6   1 Corinthians 10:31
Day 7   2 Corinthians 4:16-18

Week 40

Jean-Paul Sartre (1905-1980)

Sartre was extremely influential because he was so
widely read. It is my observation that more
believing Christians lose their faith during their college years by
reading Sartre (and his colleagues Camus and Kafka) than by any
other influence. When Christians read Sartre it should be with the
Bible close at hand. The allure of Sartre was the allure of modernity:
experience was the essense of reality
itself. Sartre persuasively argued that we
all have a sense of being, what he called
Being-in-Itself. We existed, then, in a
world of our own making. The world
existed because we existed. We created
the world through our decisions, actions, and behavior. The
individual, then, not an ideal, not a deity, were penultimate in Sartre's
philosophy. Morality was the measure of our ability to be ourselves.
The ramifications of this philosophy were obvious. Men were invited
to a place of intellectual self-centeredness which became the spirit of
the 20ᵗʰ century. Sartre confirmed what everyone in the post-Sigmund
Freud world suspected: people were the first, last, and only
consideration in decision making. There was no reality outside the
human will.

> People exist in a world of
> their own making.

Passage

There are two kinds of Existentialists; first, those who are Christian
and on the other hand the atheistic Existentialists, among whom I
class myself. What they have in common is that they think that
existence precedes essence, or, if you prefer, that subjectivity must be
the turning point. . . Existentialism is nothing less than an attempt to
draw all the consequences of a coherent atheistic position. It isn't
trying to plunge man into despair at all. But if one calls every attitude
of unbelief despair, like the Christians, then the word is not being used
in its original sense. Existentialism isn't so atheistic that it wears itself
out showing that God doesn't exist. Rather, it declares that even if God
did exist, that would change nothing. There you've got our point of
view. Not that we believe that God exists, but we think that the
problem of His existence is not the issue. In this sense, existentialism
is optimistic, a doctrine of action, and it is plain dishonesty for
Christians to make no distinction between their own despair and ours
and then to call us despairing. If man, as the Existentialist conceives

him, is indefinable, it is because at first he is nothing. Only afterward will he be something, and he himself will have made what he will be. Thus there is no human nature, since there is no God to conceive it. Not only is man what he conceives himself to be, but he is also only what he wills himself to be after this thrust toward existence. . . The existentialist...thinks it very distressing that God does not exist, because all possibility of finding values in a heaven of ideas disappears along with Him; there can no longer be a priori of God, since there is no infinite and perfect consciousness to think it. Nowhere is it written that the Good exists, that we must be honest, that we must not lie; because the fact is that we are on a plane where there are only men. Dostoevsky said, If God didn't exist, everything would be possible. That is the very starting point of existentialism. Indeed, everything is permissible if God does not exist, and as a result man is forlorn, because neither within him nor without does he find anything to cling to."
(Jean-Paul Sartre)

Biblical Response

To Sartre, people were the captain of their ships, masters of their fate. It is obvious that Sartre misses the whole point of the Gospel. We are saved by someone outside our experience. Our understanding of this comes through language (see Heidegger) but it certainly is not something we can do for ourselves.

> **Romans 10: 9** That if you confess with your mouth, "Jesus is Lord," and believe in your heart that God raised him from the dead, you will be saved.

Journal Writing

Sartre's view of hell is found in his play *No Exit.* In this play, three people who dislike each other intensely spend eternity together. "There's no need for red-hot pokers. Hell is--other people!" (*No Exit*) What is the end result, however, of unrepented sin? What happens to people who are not saved?

Praying Scripture

Lord, thank you that you are my Lord and Savior. Thank you that I shall spend all of eternity with you. Amen.

Further Reflection

Week 41

Simone De Beauvoir (1908-1986)

Beauvoir was an influential feminist theorist and a key 20th century spokesperson for Existentialism, a movement in philosophy that emphasized individual freedom, human experience, and subjective choice. She believed that people, especially women, must take control of the meanings which others (e.g., husbands and fathers) placed on their lives.

> She was an advocate of "free love" and completely rejected the biblical understanding of marriage, which she saw as an oppressive institution.

Passage

You see it has never been very easy for me to live, though I am always very happy. I like so much to live and I hate the idea of dying one day. And then I am awfully greedy I want everything from life, to have many friends and to have loneliness, to work much and write good books, and to travel and enjoy myself, to be selfish and to be unselfish. You see, it is difficult to get all I want. And then when I do not succeed I get mad with anger (Beauvoir).

Biblical Response

The biblical image of a perfect woman is considerably different from the nihilistic picture Beauvoir painted of herself.

> **Proverbs 31: 26-29** She speaks with wisdom, and faithful instruction is on her tongue. She watches over the affairs of her household and does not eat the bread of idleness. Her children arise and call her blessed; her husband also, and he praises her: "Many women do noble things, but you surpass them all."

Journal Writing

Do you know a Proverbs 31 woman? Describe her.

Praying Scripture

LORD, THANK YOU THAT YOU HAVE PLACED GODLY
WOMAN IN MY LIFE. HELP ME TO BE THIS SORT OF
WOMAN OR TO MARRY SUCH A PERSON. AMEN.

Further Reflection

Day 2   Malachi 4:6
Day 3   Matthew 10:37
Day 4   Ephesians 6:4
Day 5   1 Thessalonians 2:11
Day 6   Proverbs 22: 6, 15
Day 7   Proverbs 23:13-14

Week 42

John Dewey (1859-1952)

Dewey's educational theory completely transformed American education. Dewey argued that the traditional quest to learn a corpus of information based on permanent truths was a futile activity because there was no such truth. There were no immutable structures of reality. Dewey argued in favor of fallibilism which posited that nothing about the world could be logically conclusive. The only reality was experience and then practice. Truth, to Dewey, was merely the theories to which we all subscribed and mutually agreed to call "truth." Truth, then, to Dewey, was a reflection of circumstances and contingencies. Dewey rejected all organized religion, especially Christianity, that purported to know the whole and complete truth. Dewey had no problem with people living in this sort of fairyland, as long as they did not force their delusions on anyone else.

> Truth to Dewey was a reflection of circumstances and contingencies.

Passage

We have seen that a community or social group sustains itself through continuous self-renewal, and that this renewal takes place by means of the educational growth of the immature members of the group. By various agencies, unintentional and designed, a society transforms uninitiated and seemingly alien beings into robust trustees of its own resources and ideals. Education is thus a fostering, a nurturing, a cultivating, process. All of these words mean that it implies attention to the conditions of growth. We also speak of rearing, raising, bringing up -- words which express the difference of level which education aims to cover. Etymologically, the word education means just a process of leading or bringing up. When we have the outcome of the process in mind, we speak of education as shaping, forming, molding activity -- that is, a shaping into the standard form of social activity. In this chapter we are concerned with the general features of the way in which a social group brings up its immature members into its own social form (John Dewey, *Democracy and Education*).

Biblical Response

What a sterile, unhappy world it would be if things changed with such random senselessness as Dewey implies. And then to teach that to our children! The Bible insists that parents are the primary agents of education for their children. While parents may choose to share this role with the state or a private school, they must never abdicate their role.

> **Psalm 78: 4** We will not hide them from their children; we will tell the next generation the praiseworthy deeds of the Lord, his power, and the wonders he has done.

Journal Writing

What is the most important thing you learned yesterday? Think carefully before you answer.

Praying Scripture

LORD, THANK YOU THAT YOU HAVE NOT HIDDEN TRUTH FROM ME. HELP ME NOT TO HIDE THESE TRUTHS FROM MY CHILDREN; HELP ME TO TELL THE NEXT GENERATION YOUR PRAISEWORTHY DEEDS, YOUR POWER, AND THE WONDERS YOU HAVE DONE. AMEN.

Further Reflection

Day 2   1 John 5:3
Day 3   2 Corinthians 1:3-4
Day 4   2 Corinthians 4: 6-7
Day 5   2 Corinthians 4: 16-18
Day 6   2 Corinthians 5:6-8
Day 7   2 Rointhians 5:9-10

Week 43

Bertrand Russell (1872-1970)

Russell was an extremely productive writer who rejected all subjectivity. He even disavowed that there was any intrinsic through or knowledge on which a world view could be built. All reality must be subject to objective logical inquiry. Thus, psychology and other social sciences were suspect. Naturally, all religions, full of speculation and unable to be quantified, were rejected out-of-hand. If an actual event could not be quantified or repeated then it was not real. There was no reality outside of natural science or quantified history.

> If an actual event could not be quantified or repeated then it was not real.

Passage

How, in such an alien and inhuman world, can so powerless a creature as Man preserve his aspirations untarnished? A strange mystery it is that Nature, omnipotent but blind, in the revolutions of her secular hurryings through the abysses of space, has brought forth at last a child, subject still to her power, but gifted with sight, with knowledge of good and evil, with the capacity of judging all the works of his unthinking Mother. In spite of Death, the mark and seal of the parental control, Man is yet free, during his brief years, to examine, to criticise, to know, and in imagination to create. To him alone, in the world with which he is acquainted, this freedom belongs; and in this lies his superiority to the resistless forces that control his outward life (Bertrand Russell, "A Free Man's Worship").

Biblical Response

The idea that life is based on empiricism, rationality, quantified truth of any sort, is absurd. Honestly, how does one measure hope? Love? Faith? And what is life without those things?

> **Romans 5:3-5** Not only so, but we also rejoice in our sufferings, because we know that suffering produces perseverance; perseverance, character; and character, hope. And hope does not disappoint us, because God has poured out his love into our hearts by the Holy Spirit, whom he has given us.

Journal Writing

Describe an experience, perhaps a miracle, that has happened to you and cannot be explained by any rational means.

Praying Scripture

LORD, I REJOICE IN MY SUFFERINGS, BECAUSE I KNOW THAT SUFFERING PRODUCES PERSEVERANCE; PERSEVERANCE, CHARACTER; AND CHARACTER, HOPE. AND HOPE DOES NOT DISAPPOINT ME, BECAUSE YOU POURED OUT YOUR LOVE INTO MY HEARTS BY THE HOLY SPIRIT, WHOM YOU HAVE GIVEN ME. AMEN.

Further Reflection

Day 2   Ezekiel 36:26-29
Day 3   Romans 7:6, 24-25
Day 4   Romans 12:2
Day 5   1 Corinthians 1:9, 24, 30
Day 6   1 Corinthians 2: 12, 14-16
Day 7   1 Peter 2:3, 9

Week 44

John Stuart Mill (1806-1873)

Though Mill was a 19th century philsopher, he had more of an impact on the 20th century than the 19th. Mill was the founder of Utilitarianism. Utilitarianism placed individual interest and happiness (whatever that was) at the foundation of all philosophical discussions. The individual, in other words, was paramount. Good government honored and even increased personal liberty. "We ought to do what is good for the most folks," pretty well summarizes Mill's philosophy.

> To Mill, the individual and his needs were paramount.

Passage

The struggle between Liberty and Authority is the most conspicuous feature in the portions of history with which we are earliest familiar, particularly in that of Greece, Rome, and England. But in old times this contest was between subjects, or some classes of subjects, and the government. By liberty, was meant protection against the tyranny of the political rulers. The rulers were conceived (except in some of the popular governments of Greece) as in a necessarily antagonistic position to the people whom they ruled. They consisted of a governing One, or a governing tribe or caste, who derived their authority from inheritance or conquest; who, at all events, did not hold it at the pleasure of the governed, and whose supremacy men did not venture, perhaps did not desire to contest, whatever precautions might be taken against its oppressive exercise. Their power was regarded as necessary, but also as highly dangerous; as a weapon which they would attempt to use against their subjects, no less than against external enemies. To prevent the weaker members of the community from being preyed upon by innumerable vultures, it was needful that there should be an animal of prey stronger than the rest, commissioned to keep them down. But as the king of the vultures would be no less bent upon preying upon the flock than any of the minor harpies, it was indispensable to be in a perpetual attitude of defence against his beak and claws. The aim, therefore, of patriots, was to set limits to the power which the ruler should be suffered to exercise over the community; and this limitation was what they meant by liberty. It was attempted in two ways. First, by obtaining a recognition of certain immunities, called political liberties or rights, which it was to be regarded as a breach of duty in the ruler to infringe, and which, if he did infringe, specific resistance, or general rebellion, was held to be justifiable. A second, and generally a later expedient, was the establishment of constitutional checks; by which the consent of the community, or of a body of some sort supposed to represent its interests, was made a necessary condition to some of the more important acts of the governing power. To the first of these modes of limitation, the ruling power, in most European countries, was compelled, more or less, to submit. It was not so with the second; and to attain this, or when already in some degree possessed, to attain it more completely, became everywhere the principal object of the lovers of liberty. And so long as mankind were content to combat one enemy by another, and to be ruled by a master, on condition of being guaranteed more or less efficaciously against his tyranny, they did not carry their aspirations beyond this point (John Stuart Mill, *On Liberty*).

Biblical Response

Christians understand that true freedom and liberty only come in relationship to God through Jesus Christ. It is bought at great cost and cannot be picked up at the ontological supermarket where Mill shops.

Galatians 5:1 It is for freedom that Christ has set us free. Stand firm, then, and do not let yourselves be burdened again by a yoke of slavery.

Journal Writing

Are there things, television, fashion, money, for example, that control you? How can you stop this from happening?

Praying Scripture

GOD, I THANK YOU THAT CHRIST HAS SET ME FREE. HELP ME TO STAND FIRM AND NOT LET MYSELF BE BURDENED AGAIN BY A YOKE OF SLAVERY. AMEN.

Further Reflection

Day 2   Ezra 8:23

Day 3   Daniel 9:3-5, 9-10
Day 4   Matthew 6:9-10
Day 5   Psalm 4:6
Day 6   Psalm 85:4-7
Day 7   Psalm 138:8

Week 45

Max Weber (1864-1920)

In his seminal work *The Protestant Ethic and the Spirit of Capitalism* Weber argued that capitalism developed in the West because of the predominance of Protestantism. Protestantism dominated the governments and culture of Western Europe during the times in which modern culture developed. The notion that God was pleased with hard work and frugal living assured a healthy maturation of society in a time when dislocation and poverty could have short-circuited the development of modernity.

> The notion that God was pleased with hard work and frugal living assured a healthy maturation of society.

Passage

The emancipation from economic traditionalism appears, no doubt, to be a factor which would greatly strengthen the tendency to doubt the sanctity of the religious tradition, as of all traditional authorities. But it is necessary to note, what has often been forgotten, that the Reformation meant not the elimination of the Church's control over everyday life, but rather the substitution of a new form of control for the previous one. It meant the repudiation of a control which was very lax, at that time scarcely perceptible in practice, and hardly more than formal, in favour of a regulation of the whole of conduct which, penetrating to all departments of private and public life, was infinitely burdensome and earnestly enforced. The rule of the Catholic Church, "punishing the heretic, but indulgent to the sinner", as it was in the past even more than today, is now tolerated by peoples of thoroughly modern economic character, and was borne by the richest and economically most advanced peoples on earth at about the turn of the fifteenth century. The rule of Calvinism, on the other hand, as it was enforced in the sixteenth century in Geneva and in Scotland, at the turn of the sixteenth and seventeenth centuries in large parts of the Netherlands, in the seventeenth in New England, and for a time in England itself, would be for us the most absolutely unbearable form of ecclesiastical control of the individual which could possibly exist. That was exactly what large numbers of the old commercial aristocracy of those times, in Geneva as well as in Holland and England, felt about it. And what the reformers complained of in those areas of high economic development was not too much supervision of life on the part of the Church, but too little. Now how does it happen that at that time those countries which were most advanced economically, and within them the rising citizen middle classes, not only failed to resist this unexampled tyranny of Puritanism, but even developed a heroism in its defence? For citizen classes as such have seldom before and never since displayed heroism. It was "the last of our heroisms", as Carlyle, not without reason, has said (Max Weber, *The Protestant Ethic and the Spirit of Capitalism*).

Biblical Response

> **1 Corinthians 9: 5-7** Don't we have the right to take a believing wife along with us, as do the other apostles and the Lord's brothers and Cephas? Or is it only I and Barnabas who must work for a living? Who serves as a soldier at his own expense? Who plants a vineyard and does not eat of its grapes? Who tends a flock and does not drink of the milk?

Journal Writing

If you have a job, describe what you do, how you feel about it, and how you think God responds to your work.

Praying Scripture

GOD, THANK YOU FOR YOUR GENEROUS PROVISION. I HAVE MORE THAN I NEED TO LIVE. HELP ME TO BE AS GENEROUS WITH OTHERS AS YOU ARE WITH ME. AMEN.

Further Reflection

Day 2   Psalm 37:3
Day 3   Psalm 90:17
Day 4   Deuteronomy 6:25
Day 5   Ezekiel 18:5-9
Day 6   Matthew 6:1-4
Day 7   Romans 2:13

Week 46

Ludwig Wittgenstein (1889-1951)

Wittgenstein was the Albert Einstein of Western Philosophy. As Einstein completely transformed physics, Wittgenstein transformed philosophy. In fact, some scholars argued that by introducing new paradigms and categories for discussion, he ended philosophy as a viable discipline. Like Martin Heidegger, he argued that reality was merely language. If a person could not say it, then it was not real. In other words, philosophy was irrelevant. Only language was relevant. While Western philosophy purported to discuss essential foundations of justice, reality, and ethics, these were, according to Wittgenstein, false problems distracting people from the real issues. Philosophy

> If a person could not speak it, it was not real.

tried to push people beyond their language. For example, Plato's forms were irrelevant abstractions because no one could really articulate what he meant by a "form." Mankind, Wittgenstein argued, was captured in the reality of language. If he could not speak or describe it then it was not real. This had profound ramifications on Western philosophy and made Wittgenstein one of the early leaders of a post-modernism. Post-modernism is a philosophy that argues that there is no objective theory of knowledge and truth.

Passage

Our language can be seen as an ancient city: a maze of little streets and squares, of old and new houses, and of houses with additions from various periods; and this surrounded by a multitude of new boroughs with straight regular streets and uniform houses (Ludwig Wittgenstein).

Which came first - the idea or the language?

Biblical Response

To be confined to a world that we can see and hear, in a world that is concrete, that is quantifiable, is a scary thought. In reality, Christians serve a God who will not be limited by our minds. For Wittgenstein, truths were limited by the ability to express them verbally and by the relative degree of agreement that exists to verify them. We can be

106

thankful that we serve a God who is not limited by our flawed and petty understanding of His purposes and character.

Revelation 21: 5-7 He who was seated on the throne said, "I am making everything new!" Then he said, "Write this down, for these words are trustworthy and true." He said to me: "It is done. I am the Alpha and the Omega, the Beginning and the End. To him who is thirsty I will give to drink without cost from the spring of the water of life. He who overcomes will inherit all this, and I will be his God and he will be my son.

Journal Writing

One result of Wittgenstein's theories, which more or less have been embraced by most Americans, is that theology is experiential but not confessional. Everyone wants to tell his "story." It does not matter what his confession of faith is--what matters is that he tells stories and that he listens sympathetically to others' stories. No standard exists from which most Americans measure truth. Thus, we all become quasi-therapists sympathetically listening to our problems with no real solutions to our problems. What is your confession of faith?

Praying Scripture

GOD, I AM THANKFUL THAT BECAUSE YOU MAKE ALL THINGS NEW, I CAN COME TO YOU TO QUENCH MY SPIRITUAL THIRST. PLEASE HELP ME TO BE AN OVERCOMER. AMEN.

Further Reflection

Day 2   Romans 16:25-26
Day 3   Acts 2:38
Day 4   Romans 10:3-9
Day 5   1 Timothy 3:16
Day 6   2 Timothy 1:9-10
Day 7   2 Timothy 2:13-14

Week 47

Richard Rorty (1931-)

Agreeing with Wittgenstein, Rorty is an advocate of linguistic philosophy, believing that the careful analysis of language can provide answers to most philosophical questions. To Rorty, there is nothing ubiquitous about philosophy. It is merely one more topic of conversation among curious spectators. One could just as easily be talking about the weather of the score of the latest ball game. The notion that religious people had some privileged knowledge that would help mankind is ludicrous to Rorty. On the contrary, religion to Rorty is no more than "what we do with our aloneness." Truth to Rorty is what we all agree is truth and what we agree is truth is more a reflection of circumstances than it is any absolute or objective reality outside mankind's experience. In other words, Plato, Socrates, and Aristotle, are all irrelevant because the language describing their views is archaic and dead. Rorty's assumes that he can ameliorate misguided Theists by therapeutic philosophical arguments that will cure them of the notion that they

> Truth to Rorty is what we all agree is truth and what we agree is truth is more a reflection of circumstances than it is any absolute or objective reality outside mankind's experience.

have a corpus of knowledge (i.e., Bible) that is superior to all other sources of knowledge. His conclusion is contradictory to his own beliefs, since Christians base their faith in Christ as presented through the language of the written Word of God.

Passage

If I have concrete specific doubts about whether one of my beliefs is true, I can resolve those doubts only by asking whether it is adequately justified--by finding and assessing additional reasons pro and con. I cannot bypass justification and confine my attention to truth. The difference between true beliefs considered as useful nonrepresentational mental states and as accurate representations of reality, seemed to make no difference to practice (Richard Rorty).

Biblical Response

When my children were young, I would confront them with a problem. If they exhausted all rational arguments, inevitably they would say, "My statement is true because I say it is true." When one reads Rorty and other Post-moderns, one feels that they have created a system of theory/truth whose only basis of truth is that they believe their theories with fervency and sincerity. That does not make them true, however. Not by a long shot.

> **Isaiah 6: 5-8** "Woe to me!" I cried. "I am ruined! For I am a man of unclean lips, and I live among a people of unclean lips, and my eyes have seen the King, the LORD Almighty." Then one of the seraphs flew to me with a live coal in his hand, which he had taken with tongs from the altar. With it he touched my mouth and said, "See, this has touched your lips; your guilt is taken away and your sin atoned for." Then I heard the voice of the Lord saying, "Whom shall I send? And who will go for us?" And I said, "Here am I. Send me!"

Journal Writing

I have a childhood friend who attended a movie with me entitled *Superman* (the 1950ish version). Inspired by the exploits of our hero, we returned home later that Saturday afternoon and pretended to be Superman. We stood together on the top edge of my friend's barn and proclaimed to all the world that we were in fact the cousins of Superman and that we also could fly. While we knew we were not really his cousins, we sincerely believed we could fly; We were committed to that belief, we spoke that truth with our language. It was real to us. I graciously offered to allow my friend to jump first. He hurt himself pretty badly. Describe an incident where you sincerely made a bad choice and describe the consequences. What did you learn?

Praying Scripture

GOD, WOE TO ME! I AM RUINED! FOR I AM A MAN OF UNCLEAN LIPS, AND I LIVE AMONG A PEOPLE OF UNCLEAN LIPS, AND MY EYES HAVE SEEN YOU THE KING, THE LORD ALMIGHTY. I HAVE NOT MET ANY ANGELS, BUT I AM WILLING TO BE USED BY YOU, FATHER. HERE AM I. SEND ME! AMEN.

Further Reflection

Week 48

Alfred North Whitehead (1861-1947)

First the good news. The agnostic Whitehead believed in God--if a decidedly anemic God. Opposing Existentialists and Naturalists, Whitehead preferred to work within society's institutions. The bad news is Whitehead appealed to direct experience. Like other Romantics, he saw harmony in nature and in human experience. Like some of the Empiricists, Whitehead leaned toward rationalism. Whitehead abandoned the notion, strong in Western philosophy since Plato, that what is most unchanging is most real. Instead he conceived the structure of reality in dynamic terms. Reality was not based on Platonic "forms" but on "fluid experience." The emphasis was on becoming, on development in time, rather than on static being, and by implication, absolute truth. Whitehead embraced the modernist notion of process thought. The central metaphor for process thought is that of organism, rather than that of machine. The formation of each event is a function of the nature of the entities involved. Whitehead's agnosticism was most evident in his understanding of suffering. God "the fellow-sufferer who understands," who does not coerce but merely seeks to persuade other beings in the direction of love, seemed profoundly attractive in the light of the Jewish Holocaust. Process schemes abandoned the notion of an omnipotent God, because only a wimpish God would allow six million people to die.

> The agnostic Whitehead believed in God--if a decidedly anemic God.

Passage

God is creative in the only sense in which creation is given any meaning by our experience. To create is to mold the course of events into correspondence with an idea. Men thus literally create each other when they mold each other's character by education and friendship. Thus the paradoxes of timeless purpose, together with those of non-sensitive ("impassive") love, and of action without reaction, are done away with once for all (Alfred Lord Whitehead).

Biblical Response

God is everywhere, all the time, and in absolute control.

> **Psalm 36:5-9** Your love, O Lord , reaches to the heavens, your faithfulness to the skies. Your righteousness is like the mighty mountains, your justice like the great deep. O Lord , you preserve both man and beast. How priceless is your unfailing love! Both high and low among men find refuge in the shadow of your wings. They feast on the abundance of your house; you give them drink from your river of delights. For with you is the fountain of life; in your light we see light.

Journal Writing

Write about a time when God protected you from an incident that could have been harmful.

Praying Scripture

YOUR LOVE, O LORD , REACHES TO THE HEAVENS, YOUR FAITHFULNESS TO THE SKIES. YOUR RIGHTEOUSNESS IS LIKE THE MIGHTY MOUNTAINS, YOUR JUSTICE LIKE THE GREAT DEEP. O LORD , YOU PRESERVE BOTH MAN AND BEAST. HOW PRICELESS IS YOUR UNFAILING LOVE! BOTH HIGH AND LOW AMONG MEN FIND REFUGE IN THE SHADOW OF YOUR WINGS. THEY FEAST ON THE ABUNDANCE OF YOUR HOUSE; YOU GIVE THEM DRINK FROM YOUR RIVER OF DELIGHTS. FOR WITH YOU IS THE FOUNTAIN OF LIFE; IN YOUR LIGHT, I SEE LIGHT.   AMEN.

Further Reflection

Day 2   Matthew 3:1-10
Day 3   Matthew 18:21-35
Day 4   Matthew 20:1-16
Day 5   Acts 7:54-8:8
Day 6   1 Kings 19:1-8
Day 7   Psalm 42

Week 49

Jacques Derrida (1930-)

Derrida argue that humans create reality through language. Although Western culture has tended to assume that speech is a clear and direct way to communicate, Derrida questions this assumption. The author's intentions in speaking cannot be unconditionally accepted. Therefore, if language is imprecise, then everything is up for grabs. Much like Wittgenstein, Derrida argued that most of us merely play language games. Every utterance is a move in a language game. Thus, reality is organic and always changing. At the same time, there emerged a dualism between reality and superstition. This dualism, as old as the Greek discussion of mythology (i.e., superstition) vs. logos (i.e., reality), created a tension that exists until today. Derrida called this logocentricism. As a child will tie a line of string to a ball and whirl it around his head, Western society settles in its logos (language/ word) and whirls all sorts of theories around its head. These theories–about what is right or wrong, good and bad–maintain their integrity only so long as the string holds to the logos. If that breaks, the balls–and dualistic notions–fly out into the cosmos. This whole process is called deconstruction which is concerned with talking about the relationship of the ball to the string to the logos.

> Derrida argued that most of us merely play language games. Every utterance is a move in a language game.

Passage

"What does it mean that for 30 years it was said something is dead?" Mr. Derrida asked. "If the eulogies continue for 30 years, does it mean that something is dead? Or does that not mean something is not dead?" (Jacques Derrida)

Biblical Response

Words are important to a Christian but they are not what makes something exist. God is the creator and he shares His role with no one.

> **Zechariah 12: 1-5** This is the word of the LORD concerning Israel. The Lord , who stretches out the heavens, who lays the foundation of the earth, and who forms the spirit of man within him, declares: "I am going to make Jerusalem a cup that sends all the surrounding peoples reeling. Judah will be besieged as well as Jerusalem. On that day, when all the nations of the earth are gathered against her, I will make Jerusalem an immovable rock for all the nations. All who try to move it will injure themselves. On that day I will strike every horse with panic and its rider with madness," declares the Lord. "I will keep a watchful eye over the house of Judah, but I will blind all the horses of the nations.   Then the leaders of Judah will say in their hearts, 'The people of Jerusalem are strong, because the Lord Almighty is their God.'

Journal Writing

Tell about a prayer you prayed and how God answered it.

Praying Scripture

God, keep a watchful eye over me. Protect me from my enemies. Let people say about me, "He is strong because the Lord Almighty is his God." I will be careful to give you all the glory. Amen.

Further Reflection

Day 2   John 17:1-5
Day 3   Romans 8:18-30
Day 4   Acts 2:14, 22-24
Day 5   Revelation 1:4-8
Day 6   Psalm 2
Day 7   John 20:19-31

Week 50

Jean Baudrillard (1929-)

Braudrillard coins a term "hyperreality" that captures the essence of his philosophy. Hyperreality referred to the virtual and resulting unreal power of contemporary culture in an age of influential mass media. Reality, then, to Baudrillard, is not necessarily defined by human language: it is defined by the public media. Reality is defined by an external reality–the opposite of orthodox Existentialism. He is particularly critical of America, whose dominating culture is pure banality. America is full of facile people who do not know what is real and what is purported to be real by the mass media. This boogey man, the mass media, seduces people into a sort of mindless stupor. In the midst of all this superficiality, good and evil are irrelevant. One simply cannot walk through the maze of modern culture to know what is right and what is wrong.

> Reality to Baudrillard, is not necessarily defined by human language: it is defined by the public media.

Passage

Can one ask questions about the strange fact that, after several revolutions and a century or two of political apprenticeship, there are still a thousand persons who stand up and twenty million who remain 'passive'--and not only passive, but who, in perfectly good faith and without even asking themselves why, frankly prefer a football match to a human and political drama? (Jean Baudrillard)

Biblical Response

God's Word is not without drama. It is more captivating than any televison show.

> **Daniel 7:9-10** As I looked, thrones were set in place, and the Ancient of Days took his seat. His clothing was as white as snow; the hair of his head was white like wool. His throne was flaming with fire, and its wheels were all ablaze. A river of fire was flowing, coming out from before him. Thousands upon thousands attended him; ten thousand times ten thousand stood before him. The court was seated, and the books were opened.

Journal Writing

Some scholars argue that watching too much television results in shallow thinking. This may cause viewers to resist or to abandon the spoken word. Write your reaction to that statement. During the coming week, log how many hours you watch television. Consider whether the number is too high.

Praying Scripture

GOD, YOU ARE MIGHTY AND AWESOME. I PRAISE AND GLORIFY YOU. YOU DO NOT NEED TO DO ANYTHING FOR ME. I SIMPLY ENJOY BEING IN YOUR PRESENCE, FATHER. ACCEPT MY PRAISE OFFERING IN JESUS' NAME. AMEN.

Further Reflection

Day 2   Exodus 16:2-15
Day 3   Romans 11:13-16
Day 4   Jeremiah 20;7-13
Day 5   Psalm 10:12-18
Day 6   Luke 12:49-56
Day 7   Matthew 8:1-4

Week 51

Jurgen Habermas (1929-)

Habermas has resurrected the works of Plato and other metaphysicists and has taken philosophy away from language and communication and has taken it back to a discussion of rationality. Truth, Habermas argued, may yet be discovered outside normal human experience. He points out that our wholesale replacement of ethics and religious values with human subjectivity and experience has had a devastating effect. He is not suggesting nor hoping that the world will experience a revival. He merely suggests, as Nietzsche had, that the vacuum created by the absence of absolute truth and authority would have a devastating effect on world culture. And, indeed, both of these men are right. Habermas argues that we should all work harder at developing consensus instead of abandoning the social structures that have given Western culture life. He, as it were, has brought the Enlightenment back into discussion and suggested that modernity still had a lot to be desired especially as it applies to Post-modernity.

> Habermas has resurrected the works of Plato and other metaphysicists and has taken philosophy away from language and communication and has taken it back to a discussion of rationality.

Passage

Political culture arises out of delicate networks of mentalities and convictions which cannot be generated by or simply steered through administrative measures. What we lament is the handling without hindsight of imponderable and rest-worthy moral and spiritual resources which can only regenerate spontaneously, and not by decree. The self-understanding, the political self-consciousness of a nation of citizens of the State forms itself through the medium of public communication. And this communication is founded on a cultural infrastructure (Jurgen Habermas).

Biblical Response

God also seeks to speak, to reason with His people.

> **Isaiah 1:18-19** "Come now, let us reason together," says the Lord. "Though your sins are like scarlet, they shall be as white as snow; though they are red as crimson, they shall be like wool. If you are willing and obedient, you will eat the best from the land.

Journal Writing

If there is a sin your life that needs to be confessed to the Lord, write your confession and ask His forgiveness. Let yourself be made as white as snow.

Praying Scripture

God, though my sins are like scarlet, please make them as white as snow; though they are red as crimson, make them like wool. I am willing and I will try to be obedient so I may eat the best from the land.

Further Reflection

Day 2   Jeremiah 31:31-34
Day 3   Hebrews 5:7-10
Day 4   Philippians 3:8-14
Day 5   Psalm 126
Day 6   John 12:1-8
Day 7   Matthew 16:21-28

Week 52

Viktor E. Frankl (1905-1997)

The ancient Greeks began the noble pursuit of truth 500 years before Christ was born. At first, they spoke of goodness, virtue, and justice. By the 21th century most philosophers abandoned that quest and embraced pragmatism, post-modernism, hyperreality, determinism, dialecticism, and logo-centricism. Reality lay in the human heart and human experience, for sure, but there was no better world outside for which mankind could reach. In other words, since the clear vision of Plato, mankind became lost in the cosmos. Man was now the result of a purposeless and materialistic process that did not have him in mind. Discovery that the universe lacked any purpose or plan had the inevitable corollary that the workings of the universe

> Man was now the result of a purposeless and materialistic process that did not have him in mind.

could not provide any automatic, universal, eternal, or absolute criteria of right and wrong. Frankl, in his own way, called his society back to a land beyond the cold, unappetizing wilderness of post-modernism. Frankl, himself a survivor of Nazi concentration camps, observed that inmates who had hope survived while those who did not died. Hope, therefore, was crucial to survival. Frankl wrote "A man who could not see the end of his 'provisional existence' was not able to aim at an ultimate existence." Quoting Nietzsche, Frankl was fond of saying "he who has a *why* to live can bear with almost any *how*." Within the philosophical perimeters presented in the last weeks, where was there any hope? No where. Unfortunately Frankl asked all the right questions but had no real answers.

Passage

Ultimately, man should not ask what the meaning of his life is, but rather must recognize that it is *he* who is asked. In a word, each man is questioned by life; and he can only answer to life by *answering for* his own life; to life he can only respond by being responsible (Viktor Frankl).

Biblical Response

Jesus Christ is the Way, the Truth, and the Life. That is the bottom-line answer to the questions that people have asked for the past 4000 years.

> **Isaiah 55:8-9** "For my thoughts are not your thoughts, neither are your ways my ways," declares the Lord. As the heavens are higher than the earth, so are my ways higher than your ways and my thoughts than your thoughts."

Journal Writing
Describe a worthwhile but seemingly impossible task and write a prayer asking God to accomplish it.

Praying Scripture
GOD, I KNOW MY THOUGHTS ARE NOT YOUR THOUGHTS, NEITHER ARE YOUR WAYS MY WAYS. AS THE HEAVENS ARE HIGHER THAN THE EARTH, SO ARE YOUR WAYS HIGHER THAN MY WAYS AND YOUR THOUGHTS THAN MY THOUGHTS. HELP ME MAKE YOUR THOUGHTS AND YOUR WAYS, MY THOUGHTS AND WAYS. AMEN.

Further Reflection
Day 2   Psalm 131:1
Day 3   Psalm 19:13
Day 4   Job 37:24
Day 5   Proverbs 13:10
Day 6   Proverbs 15:5, 10, 12, 55
Day 7   1 Corinthians 3:18

Credits, Permissions, and Sources

Most of the literature cited in this book is in the public domain. Much of it is available on the Internet, through the following sites:

All graphics are copyrighted by Clipart.com.

Michael Albert, " Richard Rorty the Public Philosopher" (http://www.zmag.org/rortyphil.htm)
> Richard Rorty, *Truth and Progress*

Aristotle, *Nicomachean Ethics*, translated by W. D. Ross

Batleby.com, Great Books Online
> Marcus Aurelius, *Meditations*
> George Berkeley, *Three Dialogues Between Hylas and Philonous in Opposition to Sceptics and Atheists* Thomas Hobbes, *Laviathan*
> David Hume, *An Enquiry Concerning Human Understanding*
> Immanuel Kant, *Fundamental Principles of the Metaphysic of Morals*
> John Locke, *Some Thoughts Concerning Education*
> John Stuart Mill, *On Liberty*
> Jean Jacques Rousseau, *On the Inequality among Mankind*

Bartlett's Quotations, 1919
> Diogenes' Quotes

Bulfinch's Mythology (http://www.bulfinch.org/fables/bull1.html)

John Dewey, *Democracy and Education* (http://www.ilt.columbia.edu/about/staff_list.html)

Diogenis Laertius in his 1st book "Lives and Opinions of Eminent Philosophers" Giannis Stamatellos, translator, "The Presocratic Philosophers," in The Cambridge Dictionary of Philosophy, Cambridge University Press, 1995.
> *Writings*, by Thales

Eusebius, *Prep. Ev.* 14.18.2-5, Long & Sedley

Everypoet.com

Arthur Fairbanks, ed, *The First Philosophers of Greece* (London: K. Paul,
Trench, Trubner, 1898), 132-156.
    "The Fragments of Anaxagoras"
    "Pythagoras and the Pythagoreans, Fragments and Commentary"

Viktor Frankl, *Man's Search for Meaning*
(http://www.geocities.com/~webwinds/frankl/frankl.htm)

William Godwin, *The Anarchist Writings of William Godwin* (Freedom
Press)

Jurgen Habermas, *Destruction of Reason*
(http://carbon.cudenver.edu/~mryder/itcdata/postmodern.html)

Martin Heidegger
(http://www.regent.edu/acad/schcom/rojc/mdic/martin.html)

"Hegel: Philosophy and history as theology,"
http://members.aol.com/pantheism0/hegel.htm

Heuss, Michael R. "About Friedrich Nietzsche." Great Literature Online.
    1997-2003 (http://www.underthesun.cc/Classics/Nietzsche/)
    Frederick Nietzsche, *The Anti-Christ*

"Letters from Simone de Beauvoir,"
(http://www.bbc.co.uk/works/s4/beauvoir/lett1.shtml)

Infomotions, Inc. The Alex Catalogue of Electronic Texts
(http://www.infomotions.com/alex/).

Infoplease.com. 2002 Family Education Network.
(http://aolsvc.aol.infoplease.com/ipa/A0874987.html)

The Internet Classics Archive
(http://classics.mit.edu/Aristotle/poetics.1.1.html)
        Plato, *Parmenides*
        Plotinus, *The Six Enneads*
        Montaigne, *Essays*

Internet Applications Laboratory at the University of Evansville
        Plato, *Symposium*

The Library of Congress Collection (http://www.loc.gov/exhibits/gadd/)

Karl Marx, *The Communist Manifesto*
(http://www.anu.edu.au/polsci/marx/classics/manifesto.html)

Bertrand Russell, "A Free Man's Worship" (
http://www.users.drew.edu/~jlenz/brs.html)

Jean Paul Sartre, Katharena Eiermann, "The Realm of Existentialism"
(http://rd.focalex.com/popunder/)

Arthur Schopenhauer
(http://radicalacademy.com/philschopenhauer.htm#metaphysics)

Dinitia Smith, "Philosopher Gamely In Defense Of His Ideas," *New York Times*, May 30, 1998, sect. B., p. 7.

Herbert Spencer, *First Principles*
(http://www.socsci.mcmaster.ca/~econ/ugcm/3ll3/spencer/)

Thomistic Philosophy Page
(http://www.aquinasonline.com/Topics/sent1311.html)
>   Thomas Aquinas, *Whether God can be known by the Created Intellect*

University of Oregon (http://darkwing.uoregon.edu/~rbear/bacon.html)
>   Francis Bacon, *Essays*

University of the South (http://smith2.sewanee.edu/Erasmus/pof.html)
>   Erasmus, *In Praise of Folly*

University of Virginia. Browse E-Books by Author
(http://etext.lib.virginia.edu/ebooks/Wlist.html)

Alfred North Whitehead (http://websyte.com/alan/brief.htm)

Ludwig Wittgenstein (http://www.seanet.com/~john7/wittgenstein/)

University of Wisconsin—Milwaukee. The Classic Text: Traditions and Interpretations
(http://www.uwm.edu/Library/special/exhibits/clastext/clshome.htm)

Wright State University (http://philos.wright.edu/Dept/PHL/PHL.html)
>   Rene Descartes, *Meditation II*, Translated by John Veitch (1901)

- Notes -